technical EXPERT

Technik

Workbook
mit Mediensammlung

von
Andrea Eder-Panev
Arnd Nadolny
Rachel Herring

Ernst Klett Verlag
Stuttgart · Leipzig · Dortmund

Trackliste

TOPIC	TRACK	PLAYING TIME
1	**A1** Forward Thinking: Recruitment in the digital world	05:01
	A2 Technically working: Are EVs the future of our mobility?	06:14
	A3 Sustainable housing technologies	03:57
	A4 Forward Thinking: Equality and diversity in recruitment	06:15
	A5 Forward Thinking: Working abroad	05:15
	A6 Top 3 Tips Learned From 20 Internship Experts	03:20
2	**A7** Laura and Hiroto's discussion	04:15
	A8 Interview with Mazuno staff	05:06
	A9 Technically working: Green renovations	07:24
	A10 Technically working: Rise of the robots	08:31
	A11 Live Wires - How can we make UK engineering more diverse?	03:08
3	**A12** Technically working: Innovative products and services	04:15
	A13 Technically working: The future of green flying	05:06
	A14 Message from Sartaj	07:24
	A15 Technically working: Running a construction business	06:29
	A16 Technically working: Production and manufacturing software	07:14
	A17 Jason's introduction	01:55
	A18 How Paul Akers developed 800+ products	08:13
4	**A19** Why to DIY: Spray foam	04:23
	A20 Rex: Exoskeleton at Naidex	04:24
5	**A21** Communication skills	03:16
	A22 AEBS explained	03:18
	A23 Preparing to service an elevator	02:31
	A24 Hydrogen: A climate game-changer?	02:01
6	**A25** Problems at work	05:01
	A26 The four-sides model	04:24
	A27 Why to DIY: Dealing with mould and condensation	05:16
	A28 How to handle conflict at work	02:41

Gesamtlaufzeit: 02:16:17

Symbole

A1 (Lautsprecher)	Audio
→ SB p. 1	Verweis auf das Schulbuch technical EXPERT

Audios, Audioskripte und Lösungen zum Arbeitsheft online und in der App verfügbar!

1. Auf **schueler.klett.de** anmelden
2. Nutzer-Schlüssel (oder QR Code) einlösen
3. Digitale Medien online nutzen oder in die **Klett Lernen App** laden

Nutzer-Schlüssel
pE1Z-3cPm-g5gB

1 APPLICATIONS
Entering the world of work

TALKING ABOUT JOB APPLICATIONS → SB p. 15

1 Complete the crossword puzzle.

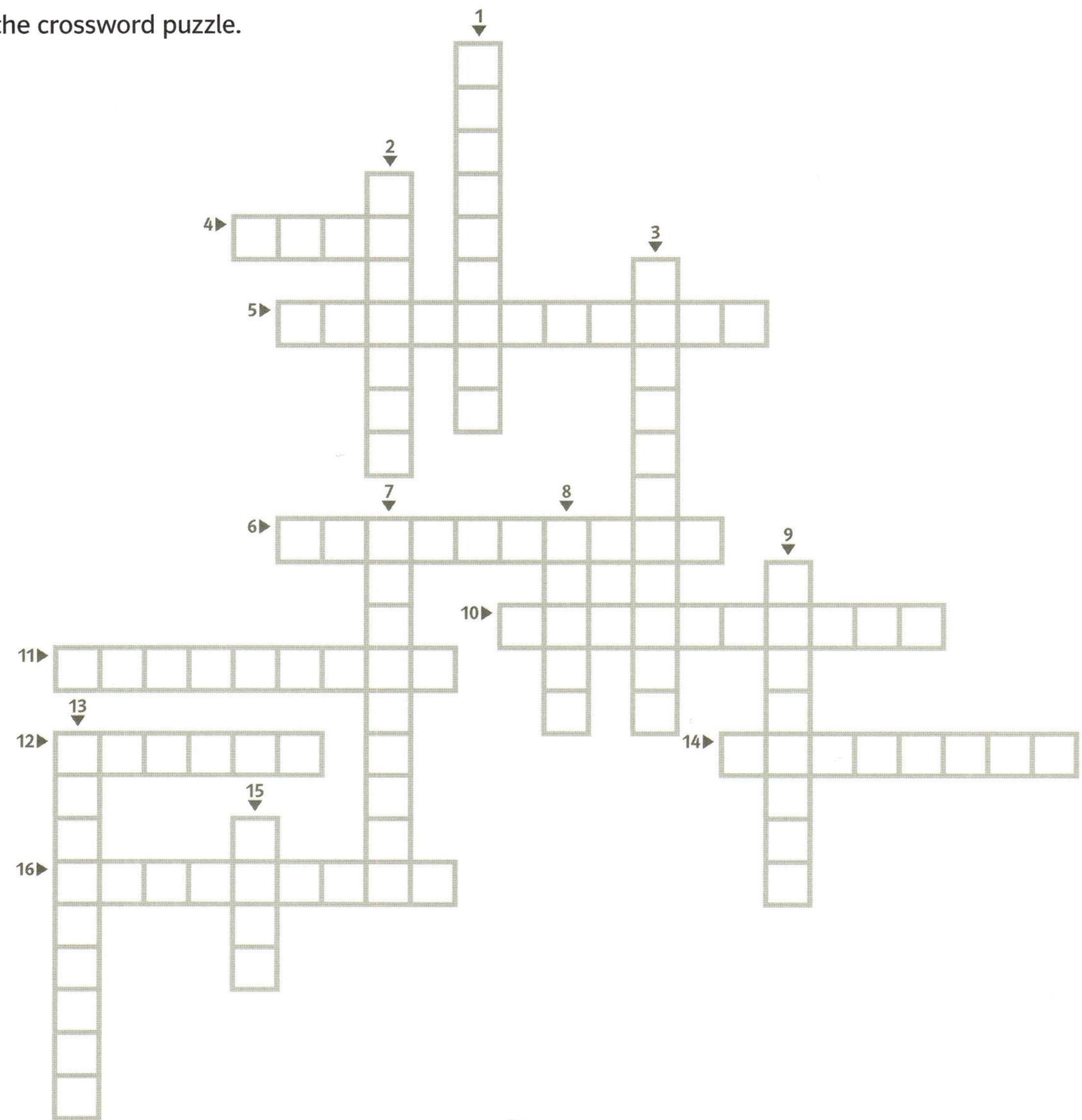

Across

4. a formal assessment to test one's knowledge
5. a document showing an achievement or qualification
6. a position within a company for students or trainees, sometimes unpaid
10. the person or people in charge of dealing with staff and decisions of greater responsibility within a company
11. a person putting themselves forward for a position
12. to give paid work to sb
14. the formal, legal agreement between an employee and employer
16. a person who works with someone else

Down

1. moving from a lower position to a higher one
2. to get better
3. to take part
7. to include
8. personnel; the people within a company's workforce
9. any person working within a company or organisation
13. the process of gaining knowledge and skills, e.g. at a school or college
15. aim; objective

2 Where necessary, add the appropriate suffix to complete these professions. You may need to change the ending of the word, while some of the words don't need to be changed at all.

-er | -ist | -or | -ant

1. analyse ______
2. instruction ______
3. manage ______
4. assistance ______
5. influence ______
6. develop ______
7. technology ______
8. direct ______
9. research ______
10. administration ______
11. special ______
12. design ______

3 Complete the table with the different forms of the words below. Then think of two more related to job applications and interviews.

Noun	Adjective	Adverb
usefulness		
		fluently
	confident	
	nervous	
punctuality		
		physically

THE ELEMENTS OF A JOB ADVERTISEMENT → SB p. 15

4 Read the job advertisement and complete the text with the missing words from the word bank.

applicants | maintenance | branches | CV | head office | staff | car dealer | qualifications | reliable | components | interest | work experience

Car Mechanics Wanted

British Sports Cars International is a leading ____________ which operates worldwide and has ____________ in 45 countries. Our ____________ is in Leeds, England, where management decides which cars are to be offered in different countries.

We are currently looking for some qualified car mechanics to join our ____________ in Manchester.

____________ should be adaptable, ____________ and have a working knowledge of English. Qualifications and ____________ in fixing vehicles and replacing vehicle parts are essential.

Further duties include inspecting the vehicle's mechanic ____________ and its engine as well as diagnosing problems with vehicles and performing ____________ checks.

If you are interested in the job, please send a ____________ and a cover letter expressing your ____________ and specifying your ____________ to Miss Claudia Ainsworth at c.ainsworth@wlsn by 24th April.

APPLICATION DOCUMENTS → SB p. 15

5 Complete the following sentences which can be used in a cover letter for a job at *Mazuno*.

1. I would like to express my interest in ____________.
2. I am currently ____________.
3. I gained work experience by ____________.
4. I also have experience ____________.
5. The job appeals to me because I believe it would ____________
____________.

JOB INTERVIEWS

→ SB p. 15

6 Use the words below to form questions that might come up in an interview in the correct tense. Then mark the box to say who would ask each of the questions – the interviewer or the candidate.

Question	Interviewer	Candidate
1. this position – to find out about – how – you ______		
2. this role – you – why – to want to do ______		
3. training opportunities – to be – to employees – there – any – available ______ ______		
4. which – to progress – opportunities – are – there ______		
5. to bring – to the job – you – what – can ______		
6. goals – to set – you – at the beginning – which – for me – would ______ ______		
7. goals – to have – you – which – for – your career ______		
8. what – strength – your – greatest – to be ______		
9. to work with – closely – colleagues – I – which ______		
10. the next steps – what – the interview process – to be – in ______ ______		

SCENARIO A

UNDERSTANDING THE SCENARIO → SB pp. 16–17

1 Use the table below to match the words and phrases from the text to their German equivalents.

1. acceleration
2. affordable
3. to be dedicated to
4. range
5. state-of-the-art
6. sustainable
7. drivetrain
8. fast-charging
9. to be committed to
10. e-mobility

A hochmodern
B schnell-ladend
C Antrieb, Antriebstechnik
D erschwinglich
E nachhaltig
F Elektromobilität
G Beschleunigung
H sich für etwas engagieren
I hier: entschlossen sein etwas zu tun
J Reichweite

1	2	3	4	5	6	7	8	9	10

2 Use information from the advertisement to complete the following sentences about *Mazuno* and what they are looking for.

1. *Mazuno* is a ______________________.
2. The company is looking for ______________________.
3. In order to make the world a better place, *Mazuno* also contributes to ______________________.
4. Applicants should have the following qualifications and skills: fluency of language, ______________________
______________________.
5. According to the advertisement, the new *Sonic* range wants to make ______________________.

3 Describe the advantages and disadvantages of online interviews with the help of the following words. Write one sentence each.

a) to save ______________________
b) equipment ______________________
c) connectivity ______________________
d) to be relaxed ______________________
____
e) impersonal ______________________
____

4 Describe the cartoon and say why or why not the applicant will get the job.

"I can hear you, can you hear me?"

TASK 1 | Making a video application → SB p. 18

A1 **5** Listen to the podcast and fill in the missing words.

1. A video application must cover the main points about the person, their ________________ and work ________________, skills and ________________.
2. The advantage of submitting an online application is that the applicant is not confined to ________________ words.
3. Before creating a video application, it's important to have a plan of what you want to say. Use ________________ or a rough ________________ to remind you of what you want to include.
4. The video should be shot in a quiet place with good ________________ and ideally with a ________________ background.
5. In the video you should speak ________________ and look ________________.
6. If the applicant is invited to an online interview, the employer provides a ________________ to an online room. Then, you both ________________ in digitally and have a conversation online.

A1 **6** Listen to the podcast and match the correct German equivalents in the word bank to the English words taken from the audio.

Anstrengung | Arbeitssuche | beschränkt | drehen | grob | Stichwörter | vorausgehen | zum Leuchten bringen

1. confined	________________	5. to shoot	________________
2. to precede	________________	6. effort	________________
3. to let shine	________________	7. prompts	________________
4. job hunting	________________	8. rough	________________

A1 7 Listen again and number Henry's tips in the order in which they are mentioned in the podcast.

- A Gather equipment ☐
- B Make a plan ☐
- C Submit it to the employer ☐
- D Shoot the video ☐
- E Share it with family or friends ☐
- F Watch it and check for mistakes ☐
- G Cut and edit the video ☐

FOCUS ON READING

→ SB pp. 19 – 21

8 Match the words from the text to their German equivalents.

1. to sift through sth (l. 2)
2. to scope sth out (l. 3)
3. to put down a deposit (l. 9)
4. to stay top of mind (l. 12)
5. to spark sb's interest (l. 14)
6. coveted (l. 18)
7. to depend on sth (l. 20)
8. to piggybank off sth (l. 20)
9. to solidify (l. 27)
10. to capitalise on sth (l. 34)

- A jds Interesse wecken
- B eine Anzahlung machen
- C immer präsent bleiben
- D festlegen, verfestigen
- E etw durchsuchen
- F auf etw angewiesen sein
- G vom Erfolg profitieren
- H begehrt
- I etw gründlich betrachten
- J aus etwas Nutzen ziehen

1	2	3	4	5	6	7	8	9	10

FOCUS ON VISUALS → SB p. 22

9 Use the following sentence starters to describe and analyse the two diagrams.

1. The upper diagram shows the factors ______.
2. The lower diagram presents the goals ______.
3. Both diagrams are set up in the form of ______.
4. In the first diagram, the two most important factors are ______, while the two least important ones are ______.
5. When choosing an influencer, ______ rank higher than ______.
6. The second diagram shows that the most important goal is ______ whereas the least important goal is ______.
7. The upper diagram indicates that ______.
8. The reason for this is that ______.
9. The second diagram makes it clear that ______.
10. All in all, it can be said that ______.

FOCUS ON MEDIATION → SB p. 23

10 Using the word bank below, choose the correct English equivalents for the German words in the list.

parking fee | supply network | battery-powered | combustion engine | wear | fossil fuels | driving ban | maintenance costs | photovoltaic power system | charging station | unsustainable

1. Parkgebühr ______
2. Verbrennungsmotor ______
3. Photovoltaikanlage ______
4. Versorgungsnetz ______
5. Verschleiß ______
6. fossile Brennstoffe ______
7. Ladestation ______
8. batteriebetrieben ______
9. umweltschädigend ______
10. Fahrverbot ______
11. Unterhaltskosten ______

FOCUS ON LISTENING → SB p. 24

A2 11 Listen to the podcast and decide whether the following statements are true or false according to what the people say. Correct the false statements.

Statement	True	False
1. Everybody's next car should be an electric car.		
2. Simon Ronay is not anti-electric car.		
3. Many people cannot afford an electric car as there is no financial support from the government.		
4. Fast charging stations take only 10 minutes to charge to 90 percent capacity of the battery.		
5. Planning journeys with electric cars becomes more difficult as it might be a problem to find charging stations in the countryside.		
6. When it's cold outside, the battery may drain more quickly.		

TASK 2 | Planning and drafting a video proposal → SB p. 25

12 Before you begin the task in your schoolbook, take some time to draft two different ideas in the table below. Then decide which is more convincing and the one you would like to go with. You can use the notes you make here to help you.

Title: ______ – ______ – ______ – ______	Title: ______ – ______ – ______ – ______
Category ______	Category ______
Strengths ______	Strengths ______
Weaknesses ______	Weaknesses ______

SCENARIO B

UNDERSTANDING THE SCENARIO → SB pp. 26–27

1 Read the website of *K&K Energy* and fill in the gaps in the following sentences with words from the word bank.

sustainability | feel obliged | priority | energy-efficient | tailored

a) *K&K's* mission is to help clients find ______________________ solutions for their buildings.

b) The consultations of the company are ________________ to the specific needs of the clients.

c) Part of *K&K's* philosophy is that they __________________ to create a more sustainable planet.

d) Achieving energy efficiency is important for increasing the ____________________ of buildings.

e) For *K&K Energy*, employee health and safety is their top _______________ .

TASK 1 | Writing a job advertisement → SB pp. 28–29

2 Using the word bank, complete the table by filling in the German translations for each of the English words listed.

authentisch | Begeisterungsfähigkeit zeigen | Diversität und Gleichberechtigung fördern | erfinderisch | faire Arbeitsbedingungen | ethisch und sozial verantwortungsbewusst | Leidenschaft für Nachhaltigkeit | gute Englischkenntnisse haben | Teamgeist haben | überzeugend | umweltbewusst | verantwortlich für eine bessere Zukunft | zuverlässig | gut darin, gleichzeitig an Projekten zu arbeiten | Kommunikationstalent

English	German
environmentally aware	
reliable	
to show enthusiasm	
innovative	
passionate about sustainability	
to have good English skills	
responsible for a better future	
fair working conditions	
authentic	
good at working on projects simultaneously	
to have team spirit	
convincing	
to encourage diversity and equality	
ethically and socially responsible	
communicative skills	

3 Match the sentence halves to form phrases that could be used in a job advertisement.

1. You will have to show enthusiasm …
2. We offer …
3. Do you have a passion …
4. Team spirit …
5. We are looking for a dynamic person …
6. The applicant must be willing to …
7. If you believe you are a suitable candidate, …

A … is required.
B … please don't hesitate to send us your application.
C … join our motivated, diverse team.
D … for sustainability and want to help people increase the sustainability of their building?
E … an interesting working environment and fair working conditions.
F … committed to reducing our ecological footprint for the benefit of a better tomorrow.
G … to be part of an ethically and socially responsible corporate structure.

FOCUS ON READING → SB pp. 31–32

4 Use the table below to match the words from the text to their definitions.

1. to orient your house (l. 6)
2. angle (l. 7)
3. insulation (l. 13)
4. hemp (l. 16)
5. to lobby for (l. 24)
6. heat pump (l. 31)
7. tap (l. 44)
8. to swap (l. 47)
9. like-minded (l. 47)
10. hydroelectric (l. 50)

A a type of plant that is used to make rope
B a piece of equipment that is used for controlling the flow of water
C to call for a change in something, e.g. the law
D to exchange
E part of a machine that takes heat from one place to another
F the space between two straight lines or surfaces joining each other
G using water flow to produce electricity
H having similar opinions and interests
I to give your house a certain direction
J the act of stopping heat from escaping

1	2	3	4	5	6	7	8	9	10

FOCUS ON LISTENING → SB p. 32

A3 **5** Listen to the five people talking about housing technologies and energy concepts. Complete the following sentences with the speakers' opinions.

Speaker 1 says that they only had a small budget to make their house more sustainable and therefore they decided to ______________________________.

Speaker 2 is in favour of renewable energy sources, but they ask that we consider that producing solar panels ______________________________.

Speaker 3 says that using high-quality windows ______________________________.

Speaker 4 thinks that it's a good idea in northern Europe to use ______________________________
______________________________.

Speaker 5 asks us to keep in mind that any homes that are built from now on should also be smart homes, which means that ______________________________.

FOCUS ON MEDIATION

→ SB pp. 34–35

7 Match the following headings of different heating systems to the corresponding ones in the text. There is one heading you do not need. Complete the table with the right headings.

A Heat easily and efficiently with environmental energy
B Environmentally friendly addition to your heating system
C Heating with renewable raw materials
D Suitable for charging your electric car
E Generate heat and electricity in your own home

Heading	Heating system
	block-type thermal power station
	heat pump
	pallet heating system charging point
	solar thermal energy

TASK 2 | Leading a job interview

→ SB pp. 35–36

A4 9 Listen to the podcast *Forward Thinking: Equality and diversity in recruitment* and answer the following questions.

1. What is Harry Ferguson's job? ____________________
2. From the perspective of an employer, what is the point of a job interview?
   ____
3. What can a candidate do if they are asked an inappropriate question?
   ____
4. What can happen to an employer if they ask an inappropriate question?
   ____
5. Write down at least three question topics which might be seen as discriminatory.
   ____
   ____
6. What is meant by legitimate questions?
   ____
7. Write down at least two question topics an employer might ask a candidate about.
   ____

SCENARIO C

UNDERSTANDING THE SCENARIO → SB pp. 37–38

1 Complete the crossword puzzle.

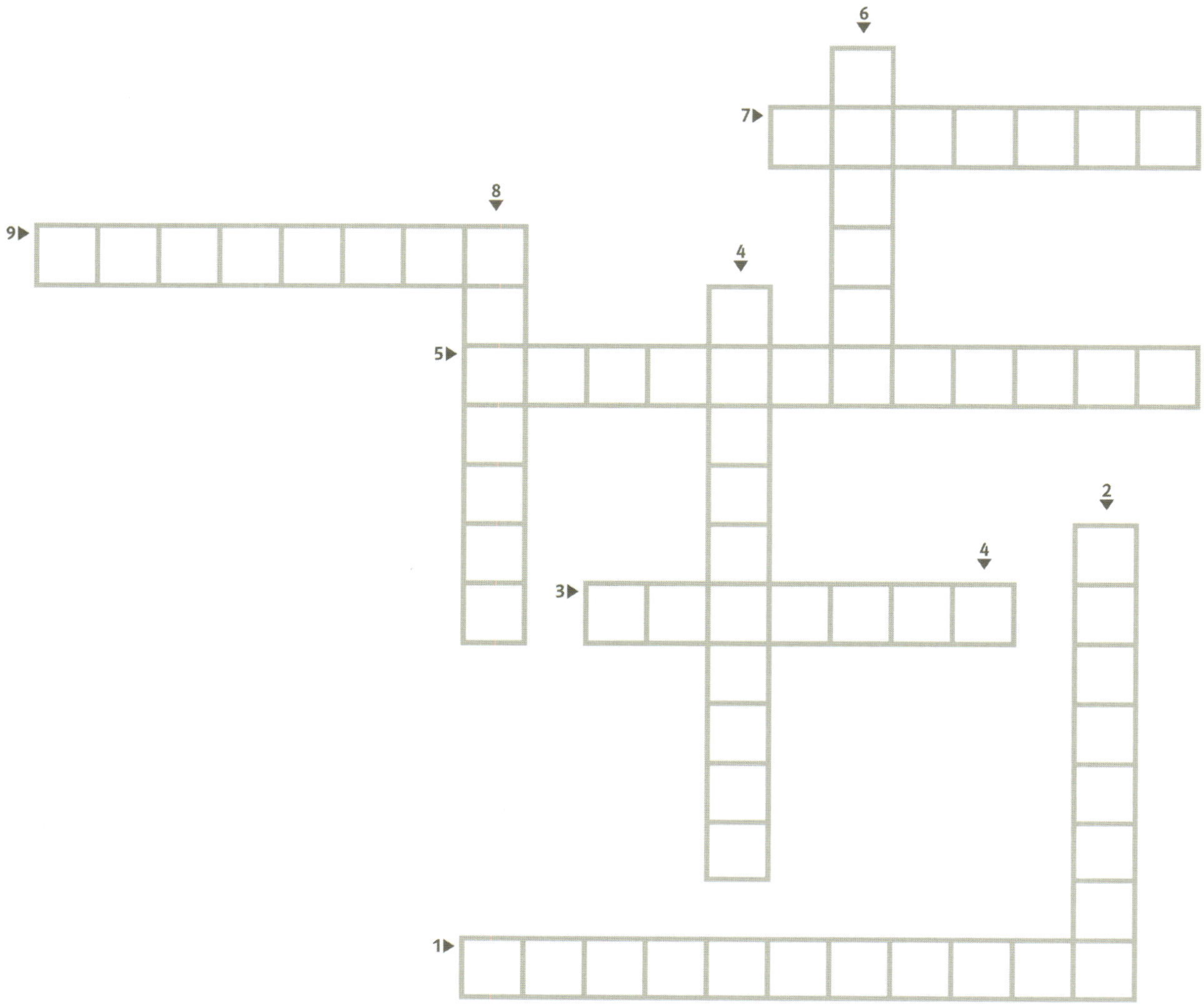

Across
1. very recent / current; modern
3. reconsider sth
5. the environment or adjacent area
7. to be indifferent towards sth
9. a moving platform for carrying passengers

Down
2. to fix up; modernise
4. a pledge or promise
6. widespread
8. to shape into a different form

TASK 1 | Writing a cover letter → SB p. 39

2 Look at the list of skills and qualities to strengthen Julia's cover letter to *VoltBlue*. Add three more skills or qualities and explain why they are important for the area of technical planning.

Skills and qualities

- flexibility
- listening skills
- organisational skills
- passion
- ______________________
- ______________________
- ______________________

____

____

____

____

____

____

____

____

____

____

____

____

____

____

FOCUS ON READING → SB pp. 40–41

3 Look at the following word snake and separate the words. Then use the words from the word snake to complete the text about the two different types of elevators.

steelropeslowrisetractionhydraulicmovinghighriseloadsinstallationpressure

______________ and ______________ elevators are the two major types of elevators. Traction elevators work with belts or ______________ and are mainly used in buildings with over 60 feet of travel as they are most energy efficient in ______________ applications.
Hydraulic elevators however use electronic pumps to push ______________ fluid into a cylinder that uses ______________. They are used in buildings with under 60 feet of travel. In contrast to traction elevators, they have lower ______________ costs and fewer ______________ parts. But they are slower and therefore mainly used in ______________ buildings for carrying heavier ______________ efficiently.

FOCUS ON MEDIATION → SB pp. 43–44

4 Use the table below to match the words and phrases from the text to their German equivalents.

1. emergency service
2. emergency power supply
3. power cut
4. appointment of date
5. safety problem
6. fine
7. emergency call button
8. to have a complete overhaul
9. supervisory authority
10. lift shaft

A Bußgeld
B Sicherheitsmangel
C Notdienst
D Notrufknopf
E Fristsetzung
F generalüberholt werden
G Stromausfall
H Notstromversorgung
I Aufzugsschacht
J Aufsichtsbehörde

1	2	3	4	5	6	7	8	9	10

FOCUS ON LISTENING → SB p. 44

A5 **5** Listen to the podcast and decide whether the following statements are true or false according to what the people say. Correct the false statements.

Statement	True	False
1. Sally Milton works as an HR manager and Orla Kelly is a careers advisor.		
2. Orla Kelly wants to attract young people from around the world to work for Cloverleaves Events.		
3. Young people who would like to work abroad must have perfect language skills.		
4. Through living abroad, young professionals can gain valuable social and cultural experiences.		
5. Applicants should find out about the social norms and laws of the country they would like to go to.		
6. In recent years, Britain has become more attractive as a workplace to EU citizens.		

FOCUS ON VISUALS → SB p. 45

6 Use the STAR method to write responses to the following interview questions.

1. Can you tell me about your experience in planning and organising?

Situation: ______________________________

____

Task: ______________________________

Action: ______________________________

____

Result: ______________________________

2. Could you give me an example of when you had to handle a stressful situation?

Situation: ______________________________

____

Task: ______________________________

Action: ______________________________

____

Result: ______________________________

____

TASK 2 | Preparing for a video interview → SB pp. 46–47

7 Look at the following tips for a video interview. Think about which part of the interview process they are important for and sort them into the table below.

- Don't sit too far from or too close to the camera
- Prepare yourself in the same way as for an in-person interview
- Pay attention to how you speak (e.g. how fast / loud)
- Dress appropriately
- Check that there is enough light in the room
- Take notes on possible questions to ask about the company / job
- Be ready for the interview at least five minutes before it starts
- Research some information about the company / job
- Make sure there are no interruptions or noises in the background
- Sit upright and look directly at the camera

In advance of the interview	Just before the interview	During the interview

8 Fill in the gaps in Julia's video interview below and recite it with a partner. You can use the hints to help you if you can't think of anything else.

Interviewer: Hello, is that Julia?

Julia: ______________________________

Interviewer: Great, well I think we should just get started. Could you tell me a little about yourself?

Julia: Of course, …

____

____

____

> **Hint:**
> - background
> - education
> - interests

Interviewer: Thank you. What made you apply for this position?

Julia: In particular, I'd like to …

____

____

> **Hint:**
> - experience
> - learn more

Interviewer: Could I ask for some more information about your academic profile?

Julia: So, firstly …

____

____

Additionally, I think it's worth mentioning that …

____

____

> **Hint:**
> - units studied
> - exam results
> - volunteer work

Interviewer: Interesting. What would you say are your greatest strengths?
What could you bring to our firm?

Julia: I would say ______________________________

____

Interviewer: Great, thank you. I also wanted to ask, do you have a special area of interest within the field?

> **Hint:**
> - people skills
> - AI technology in elevators

Julia: Actually, yes, I recently read an article on ______________________________

which helped me to learn … ______________________________

____

Interviewer: Thank you. I think that's about everything. Do you have any questions for me?

Julia: Yes, actually, I wanted to ask …

____

Interviewer: That's an interesting question, …

____

____

Does that explain everything?

> **Hint:**
> e.g. work culture, progression opportunities, post-internship positions

Julia: Yes, thank you!
Interviewer: I think that's everything now – we'll be in touch at a later date to let you know how you did.
Julia: Thank you, have a nice day, bye!

EXAM PRACTICE

Teil 1 Hörverstehen
A6 → SB p. 50

1 With whom has Alan conducted interviews? Mark the correct four options from the list.

- ☐ education experts
- ☐ healthcare professionals
- ☐ doctors, teachers and engineers
- ☐ career services personnel
- ☐ politicians
- ☐ young professionals
- ☐ college students

2 Match the terms from the podcast to their definitions.

1. faculty
2. corporate
3. executive
4. entrepeneur
5. consistently
6. to exceed
7. mindset
8. tools
9. to reciprocate

A to give the same back that is given to you
B a person who sets up their own business
C a person with high management responsibilities within a business
D again and again, without failure
E to go above and beyond
F equipment
G attitude and approach to a task or situation
H a group of associated departments within a college or university
I to do with a large company or organisation

Teil 2 Schriftliche Rezeption
→ SB pp. 50–51

Decide whether the following statements are true or false according to the information given in the text. Correct the false statements.

Statement	True	False
1. If you complete an internship abroad, your life will follow the same pattern and routine after finishing work.		
2. The cultures, attitudes and opinions will be different abroad to how they are at home.		
3. Your network won't expand as much abroad as it would at home because of language barriers.		
4. International internships should last at least six months.		
5. An internship abroad could open the possibility to working there permanently in the future.		

Teil 3 Schriftliche Produktion → SB p. 52

Complete the following sentences to use in your cover letter.

Field of work

I am currently studying ______________________ and am interested in working in ______________________ in the future. This area of work appeals to me because it involves ______________________ ______________________ and I am a ______________________.

Internship abroad

I am looking for an internship abroad because I believe that the opportunity to ______________________ ______________________ can be very ______________________ to my ______________________.

Teil 4 Mediation → SB p. 52

Number the following points to put them into the order in which they appear in the German text.

1. ☐ The trend shows that the working world is always changing; managers and personnel departments need to adapt with flexibility.
2. ☐ Gig economy workers can get jobs via online platforms and agencies.
3. ☐ The rise of gig economy workers is relatively new; in the past, people tended to work for one employer, often for their entire lives.
4. ☐ Gig economy workers often don't get paid appropriately or on time and receive less advice on how they might improve their work.
5. ☐ Gig economy workers who regularly and reliably receive work from online platforms are more motivated and better socially integrated.
6. ☐ The majority of gig economy workers are satisfied with their professional situation.
7. ☐ Gig economy workers are freelancers and self-employed people who work without fixed contracts.
8. ☐ Some people rate the gig economy as positive for workers. Others find it exploitative.
9. ☐ The gig economy emerged from the economic crisis in 2008.

Teil 5 Rollenbasierte Stellungnahme → SB p. 53

Organise the following arguments into the two categories.

- An internship is part of the standard education process.
- It increases motivation and therefore productivity.
- Interns can offer valuable skills and input, which should be rewarded.
- Many companies don't need interns. They offer placements to promote learning and development.

Interns should be paid	Interns should not be paid

2 WORKPLACE
Finding your way

TALKING ABOUT WORKPLACES → SB p. 55

1 Match the jobs with the places of work.

1. workshop
2. office
3. construction site
4. factory

A sales manager
B builder
C mechanical engineer
D production worker

1	2	3	4

JOBS IN SUSTAINABILITY → SB p. 55

2 Match the words from the podcast with their definitions.

1. 'green' jobs
2. net zero
3. previously
4. work experience
5. natural resources
6. pragmatic
7. sector knowledge
8. upskill

A before
B understanding of a particular area of industry
C something that gives you an idea of what the workplace is like, for example, an internship
D learn new skills
E where you only use as much energy as you produce
F practical, sensible, realistic
G jobs which focus on sustainability
H materials which can be found in nature

1	2	3	4	5	6	7	8

THINKING ABOUT YOUR OWN WISHES → SB p. 55

3 Write down two pros and two cons of the four different workplaces.

	Pros	Cons
workshop	• ______ • ______	• ______ • ______
office	• ______ • ______	• ______ • ______
construction site	• ______ • ______	• ______ • ______
factory	• ______ • ______	• ______ • ______

SCENARIO A

UNDERSTANDING THE SCENARIO → SB pp. 56 – 57

1 Read the email and decide whether the sentences are true or false.

Statement	True	False
1. Laura had to send a video proposal to apply.		
2. Laura has the opportunity to go to Japan.		
3. The main production facilities are in the centre of Nagoya.		
4. At the production facilties, Laura will meet some employees.		
5. The content Laura will develop is only for customers.		
6. The employment contract includes information about Laura's pay.		
7. Laura can email the contract to the company.		
8. Taka Kobayashi is the Vehicle Programme Director.		

2 Match the following words and phrases from the text with their definitions.

1. freelance
2. key members
3. timeline
4. subsistence costs
5. hard copy

A a time plan for when certain jobs should be done
B when you do work for companies or individuals, but you are not an employee
C a physical version, not a digital one
D the most important members of a team or group
E extra necessary costs, for example, food and accommodation

1	2	3	4	5

TASK 1 | Preparing questions for an interview → SB pp. 58–59

A7 **3** Listen to Laura and Hiroto Mori's conversation and choose the correct answer for each sentence.

1. The *Mazuno Sonic X* has a quick charging capacity and …

A ☐ a longer driving range.
B ☐ better heating.
C ☐ lower emissions.

2. Customers are concerned about the vehicle's …

A ☐ windows.
B ☐ manufacturing costs.
C ☐ environmental impact.

3. The company only uses aluminium which has been extracted using …

A ☐ recycled plastics.
B ☐ green energy.
C ☐ ethically sourced materials.

4. *Mazuno* invests a lot of money every year in …

A ☐ the automotive sector.
B ☐ making videos for customers.
C ☐ research and development.

5. The company uses lithium and cobalt …

A ☐ in its batteries.
B ☐ to make car doors.
C ☐ to help the environment.

6. There are regular spot checks on the mining companies to make sure …

A ☐ they are using lithium and cobalt.
B ☐ they are paying the living wage.
C ☐ they are not using child workers.

7. *Sonic X* will be on the market …

A ☐ next year.
B ☐ within the next few weeks.
C ☐ in two months.

8. Producing more vehicles will help *Mazuno* to …

A ☐ reduce overall costs.
B ☐ be environmentally conscious.
C ☐ become more stylish.

FOCUS ON READING → SB pp. 60 – 61

4 Make notes about the differences between electric vehicles and gas cars for each of these topics.

Topic	Notes
Manufacturing	______________________
Driving comparison	______________________
Fuel consumption	______________________
Fuel sourcing	______________________
Vehicle disposal and recycling	______________________

FOCUS ON VISUALS → SB p. 62

5 Complete the text with information from the diagrams.

Only ______________ of CO_2 emissions from the average conventional car are from the fuel's life cycle. This is 7 g / km more than the emissions from the fuel's life cycle of the ______________________________.

The ______________________ produces the most emissions from the fuel's life cycle. However, the other manufacturing emissions are ______________ than those of the ______________________.

The exhaust emissions of the average plug-in hybrid are the same as its ______________________.

The average electric car produces no ______________________.

FOCUS ON WRITING → SB p. 63

6 Considering environmental impacts, write about one vehicle you would like to drive and one vehicle you would not like to drive. Use the information from the text on pages 60–61 and the diagram on page 62.

FOCUS ON LISTENING → SB p. 63

A8 7 Listen to Laura's conversations with staff members in Japan and decide whether the following statements are true or false.

Statement	True	False
1. Sakura manages the payroll department.		
2. Sakura has been promoted once.		
3. *Mazuno* gets a lot of complaints from customers.		
4. A lot of the people Masato works with are from other countries.		
5. Chris is doing tests to see how heavy the new materials are.		
6. Chris studied Japanese when he was at university.		
7. Haruko has worked at *Mazuno* for sixteen years.		
8. Haruko thinks that *Mazuno* has a positive impact on the environment.		

FOCUS ON MEDIATION → SB pp. 64–65

8 Read the text and answer the questions in English.

1. Name two innovations in the automotive industry.
2. Who is involved in the vehicle production process?
3. Why do cars need to fulfil the highest quality and safety standards?
4. Which challenge are many industries currently experiencing?
5. Which four processes influence the experience of employees?
6. What advantages do virtual simulations offer to automobile manufacturers and suppliers?

TASK 2 | Planning and creating a video → SB p. 66

9 Write a video script about why the automotive industry is an exciting area to work in. Talk about:
- How the automotive industry can help the environment
- How it is growing and making use of new technology

The phrases from the word bank can help you.

The best thing about the automotive industry is … | Developments in technology mean that … | Electric vehicles can help the environment because … | Some examples of new technology in the automotive industry are … | One of the challenges the automotive industry is experiencing is … | Virtual simulations can be used to …

SCENARIO B

UNDERSTANDING THE SCENARIO → SB pp. 67–68,

1 Match the following words and phrases from the text with their definitions.

1. consultancy firm
2. retrofitted building
3. cost-benefit analysis
4. living wall
5. cutting-edge
6. smart glass
7. triple-glazed windows

A windows with three layers of glass to provide better insulation and energy efficiency
B a way of comparing the benefits and costs of a project
C a firm that provides expert advice for clients
D glass that can change how much light and heat come through it
E a building fitted with new parts that weren't available when it was built
F a wall designed to have plants growing on it
G brand new, the most advanced

1	2	3	4	5	6	7

TASK 1 | Creating an induction programme → SB p. 69

2 The new starters at *K&K Energy* have a lot of questions. Match the questions with the topics included in the induction. There are two questions for each topic.

A What happens if I am ill and can't come to work?

B Where is the canteen?

C How often are the shared spaces cleaned?

D Do you have a lot of international clients?

E Who will be my manager?

F How many employees are there at *K&K Energy*?

G What is your fire safety policy?

H How much annual leave will I get?

I Will I be working directly with clients?

J Do you offer training in specialist software?

K Is there a gym in this building?

L How do your virtual meetings work?

Induction topic	
1. Conditions of employment	
2. Health and safety	
3. Technologies	
4. *K&K Energy* and its policies	
5. Tour of the office	
6. Your role	

FOCUS ON MEDIATION → SB pp. 70–71

3 Match the words from the text with their English definitions.

1. durchschnittlich (l. 3)
2. Strom (l. 7)
3. Kilowattstunde (l. 7)
4. Haushalt (l. 11)
5. Wärmeerzeugung (l. 14)
6. Klimaanlage (l. 18)
7. erneuerbare Energieträger (l. 20)
8. Voraussetzung (l. 24)
9. Reihenhäuser (l. 25)
10. Gebäudedämmung (l. 26)
11. Zustand (l. 30)
12. feucht (l. 35)

A household
B terraced houses
C condition
D average
E air conditioning
F requirement
G kilowatt hour
H renewable energy source
I damp
J electricity
K heat generation
L insulation

1	2	3	4	5	6	7	8	9	10	11	12

4 Mediate the conversation between Tariq's colleague Clara and James, an English-speaking client who wants to know more about how buildings consume energy. Use phrases from the text to help you and use a dictionary if you need to.

James: Can I ask you a few general questions about energy consumption in homes?

You: ____________________

Clara: Ja, sehr gerne. Was wollen Sie wissen?

You: ____________________

James: What does the average energy consumption of a house include?

You: ____________________

Clara: Wärmeerzeugung macht den größten Teil aus, aber der Stromverbrauch ist auch ein wichtiger Faktor.

You: ____________________

____

James: Is heat generation the same as heating?

You: ____________________

Clara: Nicht unbedingt. Zur Wärmeerzeugung zählen auch die Bereitstellung von Warmwasser und die Erzeugung von Kälte über Klimaanlagen dazu.

You: ____________________

____

____

James: I see. That's very interesting and helpful. Thank you.

You: ____________________

____

Clara: Sehr gerne.

You: ____________________

FOCUS ON READING → SB pp. 72–74

5 Find the English words in the text that match the German words.

1. erneurbar ______________________
2. nachhaltig ______________________
3. natürliche Quellen ______________________
4. Biomasse ______________________
5. Treibhausgas ______________________
6. Solarzellen ______________________
7. frei stehend ______________________
8. Luftwärmepumpe ______________________
9. Gasheizung ______________________

6 Read the text and decide if the following statements are true, false or not in the text.

Statement	True	False	Not in text
1. Using renewable energy sources could mean that you pay less for your energy.			
2. Generating energy from coal does not produce greenhouse gases.			
3. Solar photovoltaic panels only work when it is sunny.			
4. Using solar panels for heating is cheaper than using air source heat pumps.			
5. Air source heat pumps are more sustainable than traditional oil or gas heating.			
6. Burning organic materials emits no carbon.			
7. If you live near a river, you can use a hydroelectric system to generate your electricity.			

FOCUS ON LISTENING → SB p. 74

A9 **7** Listen to the podcast and complete the summary for your colleague who wants to know more about Paul Morrison.

Paul is a ____________________. His podcast is called ____________________________ and it is about his path to living a _____________________________________. Paul lives in _____________________.

Paul has always been interested in _________________________. He stopped buying _________________ _________________ and got rid of his ______________.

________________________, he bought his own house. During his first winter in the property, he was __________________, so he decided he would have to make some _________________________.

He wanted to do all the renovations himself, so he did some research ________________ and started his podcast to document his _______________________________.

As much as _______________ of the heat in our homes is lost through the roof, so Paul used ______________________ to insulate his house. He didn't want to use a boiler powered by fossil fuels, so he decided to put in a ____________________. These are ________________________ than traditional boilers, but cheaper to run over the ____________________.

Paul says that the most important thing to do if you are building a home from scratch is to seek out an architect who ____. First, you should think about the ____, because you can use the sun's energy for _______________________________________.

You should also do your research into the ___________________________ you use. ______________________ can be a good alternative to traditional cement as the water used in the manufacturing process is ___________________________________.

FOCUS ON SPEAKING → SB p. 74

8 You are designing a new environmentally-friendly house. Describe two features you would include and explain why they are important. You can use the diagram on page 71, the text on pages 72–73 and your notes about Paul Morrison's green building project to give you some ideas.

I would install / build … | My house would (not) have … | To save energy, I would … | To generate electricity, I would use … | I think insulation is important, so I would use …

____

____

____

____

____

____

____

SCENARIO C

UNDERSTANDING THE SCENARIO → SB pp. 77–78

1 Read the email and answer the questions.

1. Who told Andrea to speak to Cem?
2. How many times have they advertised the position?
3. What two problems have there been with the candidates who have applied?
4. What has Andrea attached to the email?
5. What additional information should Cem provide?
6. When does Andrea need the first draft?
7. What is Andrea's job title?

TASK 1 | Clarifying information in a phone call → SB p. 79

2 Make questions for Cem to ask Andrea. Write one question for each topic.

1. Small talk
2. Number of candidates so far
3. Qualifications of candidates
4. Other information in application pack
5. Interviews for the position
6. Andrea's knowledge of CNC machines
7. Other information Cem can give

FOCUS ON LISTENING → SB p. 80

A10 3 Listen to the audio. Underline the wrong word and write the correct word underneath. There is one wrong word in each sentence.

1. Melissa's particular area of interest is environmentalism and its impact on the world of work.
2. The idea of robots – and automation more generally – is of course very new in many industries.
3. Industry 4.0 will improve how businesses operate and will bring huge challenges not only to companies, but their customers and employees, too.
4. The term 'Industry 4.0' can be quite simple and often seems to mean different things to different people.
5. Normally, if the machine stops working, it takes money for a new part to be ordered and delivered.
6. Better communication across all IT systems and hardware will also help improve health.
7. Engineers, technicians and robots will be needed to run these 'smart production facilities'.
8. Companies will need to be prepared to invest heavily in new advanced machinery and software, but also to train their staff.
9. Feel free to leave your idea in the comments below ...

MEDIATION → SB pp. 80–81

4 Match the words from the text with their English equivalents.

1. industrielle Revolution
2. Ungleichheit
3. vollständig
4. verringern
5. Fertigungstechnik
6. Übergang
7. datengesteuert
8. Arbeitsplätze

A complete / completely
B manufacturing technology
C transition
D jobs
E industrial revolution
F reduce
G inequality
H data driven

1	2	3	4	5	6	7	8

5 Answer the following questions in English.

1. Which four new technologies are included in Industry 4.0?
   - ______
   - ______
   - ______
   - ______
2. What is the goal of Industry 4.0?

   ______

   ______
3. What does the term Industry 4.0 describe?

   ______
4. Why is Industry 4.0 important? Give four examples.
   - ______
   - ______
   - ______
   - ______

   ______
5. What are the two potential negative impacts of Industry 4.0 for the people who work in the factories?

   ______

FOCUS ON WRITING → SB p. 81

6 How do you think workplaces will be different 50 years from now? Do you think workplaces will be better or worse than they are now? You can write about these topics:
- new technology
- robots
- the environment

______

______

______

______

______

______

______

______

______

______

______

FOCUS ON READING → SB pp. 82–85

7 Read the sentences about system integrators and underline the most suitable words for each sentence.

1. **Happily | Essentially | Unusually**, a system integrator is responsible for linking component subsystems and ensuring they work together.
2. **Alongside | Under | Because of** your colleagues, you will ensure that computer systems and networks function properly.
3. You will also produce documentation **against | installing | relevant to** system integration.
4. System integrators are **including | following | in charge of** suggesting integration options for clients.
5. You can **expect | understand | responsible** to work with lots of different clients.
6. Your **legal | training | fundamental** duties include creating user accounts and installing software.
7. You are **responsible for | communicating | voiding** meeting the needs of your clients.
8. It is **complex | verbal | critical** that you understand technical language.

8 Complete the following table with nouns, verbs and people from the same word family.

Noun	Verb	Person
integration		
	expect	–
administration		administrator
		developer
	instruct	instructor
	validate	–
collaboration		collaborator
organisation		
	define	–
		performer
communication		communicator
	manage	
	prioritise	–

TASK 2 | Writing Q&As about a job role

→ SB pp. 86–87

9 Match the questions with the answers. Write the letters in the table.

1. When did you start working here?
2. How often do you have meetings with your colleagues?
3. What is the most important skill you need for your job?
4. How often do you speak to clients?
5. What is your favourite part of your job?
6. How has your work changed since you started?
7. What do you find challenging about your job?
8. Would you like to work in this sector in the future?

A I find learning to use new software difficult.

B I have calls with clients almost every day.

C We have team meetings every week.

D I got my first job here four years ago.

E I love meeting new people and helping them solve their problems.

F There is a lot more technology in the workplace than there was when I started.

G I would like to work in this sector for a long time.

H You need to be very good at communicating.

1	2	3	4	5	6	7	8

EXAM PRACTICE

Teil 1 Hörverstehen → SB p. 90

A11 1 Listen to the audio and select the correct answers for the statements below. There can be more than one correct answer for each question.

1. Black and minority ethnic groups …
   - A ☐ are overrepresented in the student population compared to the UK population.
   - B ☐ don't often study engineering.
   - C ☐ don't progress into engineering roles as well as their white counterparts.
   - D ☐ are more likely to be unemployed after they graduate.
   - E ☐ are overrepresented in management positions in the workplace.
2. It is a disadvantage if …
   - A ☐ you have not been to a school that specialises in engineering.
   - B ☐ you don't have other people to help you get through a recruitment process.
   - C ☐ you don't know anyone else who works in the engineering industry.
   - D ☐ you go to a university in the UK.
   - E ☐ you go to an interview and don't see people like you on the other side of the desk.
3. The Graduate Engineering Engagement Programme works with …
   - A ☐ teachers.
   - B ☐ parents.
   - C ☐ underrepresented engineering students.
   - D ☐ employers.
   - E ☐ white engineering students.
4. The Graduate Engineering Engagement Programme …
   - A ☐ helps to demystify the recruitment process.
   - B ☐ helps to showcase role models.
   - C ☐ provides extra training.
   - D ☐ finds jobs for underrepresented students.
   - E ☐ helps companies to make sure there is no embedded bias in their systems.
5. To make sure your company is not excluding people for the wrong reasons, you can …
   - A ☐ make your job adverts more interesting.
   - B ☐ look at the language in your job adverts.
   - C ☐ interview more students.
   - D ☐ look at the way you do your questioning.
   - E ☐ look at who your interview panel comprises.

Teil 2 Schriftliche Rezeption → SB pp. 90–91

2 Match the words and phrases from the text with their German equivalents. Write your answers in the table below.

1. tech investment (l. 2)
2. industry-wide (l. 7)
3. male domination (l. 8)
4. misconceptions (l. 12)
5. recognise (l. 21)
6. promote (l. 22)
7. imbalance (l. 24)
8. venture capital (l. 31)

A männliche Dominanz
B Irrglauben
C Tech-Investition
D branchenweit
E Unausgeglichenheit
F Risikokapital
G befördern
H erkennen

1	2	3	4	5	6	7	8

Teil 3 Schriftliche Produktion → SB p. 91

3 At an event to help young people find careers in engineering, you speak to lots of students who have concerns about the small number of women in the tech and engineering industries. Use the information in the text to answer their questions. Write full sentences.

1. How many IT specialists in the UK are women?

____

____

2. Has the number of women in the tech sector changed over the past 10 years?

____

____

3. Why aren't women getting promoted into senior tech roles?

____

____

4. What are businesses doing to try to address gender imbalance?

____

____

5. Do women seek out employers with a strong record on diversity, equality and inclusion?

____

____

Teil 4 Mediation → SB p. 92

4 Write down key words and phrases in English for each section of the text. You do not need to write down any statistics.

1. What is important for Gen Z in their jobs

2. Gen Z wants a career with meaning

3. Gen Z has high demands

5 You have been asked to give a presentation about what is important to Gen Z in the world of work. Collect statistics from the text about each of the following aspects of work.

1. The environment
2. Material wealth
3. Work-life balance
4. Choice of employer
5. A job where they are needed
6. Social recognition
7. Leadership responsibility
8. Expertise
9. Work with meaning
10. A job for life

Teil 5 Rollenbasierte Stellungnahme → SB p. 93

6 Use the phrases you collected from the text to talk about what is most important to you in the world of work. Talk about three things that are important to you and one thing that isn't so important. Say whether you think you will have a job for life.

3 PRODUCTS AND SERVICES
Providing support

TALKING ABOUT PRODUCTS AND SERVICES → SB p. 95

1 Fill in the table by matching the examples of products and services to the correct technology sector. There are two examples for each sector.

web services | toys | digital health monitoring | recycling technology | electric vehicles | construction project scheduling | communication services | phones | medical imaging technology | wind energy technology | clothes | laptops | car engines | providing construction materials | solar photovoltaic panels | sustainable farming technology

Technology sector	Examples
1. internet software and services	
2. automotive technology	
3. consumer electronics	
4. building and construction	
5. manufacturing	
6. environmental technology	
7. energy production	
8. medical technology	

PROVIDING SUPPORT → SB p. 95

2 Think of three advantages and disadvantages of repair cafés.

Advantages:

- ______________________________
  ____
- ______________________________
- ______________________________
  ____
  ____

Disadvantages:

- ______________________________
- ______________________________
- ______________________________
  ____

THE ROLE OF TECHNOLOGY IN PRODUCTS AND SERVICES → SB p. 95

A12 3 Listen to the audio. Underline the wrong word and write the correct word underneath. There is one wrong word in each sentence.

1. Jan is fascinated by all things to do with technology and manufacturing.
2. Jan has her fitness tracker set up to alert her whenever she receives a new text.
3. It's easy to forget just how much technology has revolutionised our daily lives in a long period of time.
4. Technology is going to continue to change our everyday lives.
5. Each new technology builds on the next, and all at a faster and faster rate.
6. Additive manufacturing is a huge growth area – with the market expected to double in the next two years.
7. In healthcare, there is huge potential in a technology which allows you to create something which fits that customer exactly.
8. A huge trend across many technologies in recent years is to ensure the products and services being created are environmentally-friendly.
9. Humans have an enormous capacity to examine the world around us – and its problems – and then to come up with answers to those same problems.

SCENARIO A

UNDERSTANDING THE SCENARIO

→ SB pp. 96–97

1 Read the text and decide if the following statements are true, false or not in the text.

Statement	True	False	Not in text
1. *SAFE AVIATION* mostly works with international customers.			
2. Passenger safety is very important to the company.			
3. The product development team is working on products to make airlines more environmentally-friendly.			
4. *Royal Engines* has partnerships with lots of companies.			
5. Patented internal airflow control systems reduce the fuel consumption by 10 %.			
6. The *X1A* engine can play an important role in reducing emissions.			
7. Members of the *SAFE AVIATION* team will be at upcoming exhibitions to talk to customers.			

2 Complete the text with words from the SAFE AVIATION website.

SAFE AVIATION is one of the leading __________________ manufacturers of products for the aviation __________________. They supply various key systems such as flight __________________ systems and hydraulics which are used by major __________________ worldwide. They place great importance on __________________ safety and are regularly voted "most trusted company in the aviation sector". Another important topic for the company is __________________ change, and their product __________________ team is working on the next generation of products which will make air travel green and sustainable.

TASK 1 | Writing a product description

→ SB pp. 98–99

3 Match the questions about landing gear with the correct component parts.

1. How do you bring the aircraft to a safe stop?
2. What transfers the propulsion and braking forces between the aircraft and the ground?
3. How do you soften the impact of the aircraft's landing?
4. How do you lower and raise the landing gear into position?
5. What connects the wheels to one another?

A the shock absorber
B the tyres
C the retraction actuator
D the beam axle
E the brake assembly

1	2	3	4	5

FOCUS ON READING → SB pp. 100 – 101

4 Match the words from the text with their German equivalents.

1. comfortable
2. overheat
3. emergency landing
4. enhance
5. adjustment
6. flying conditions
7. replacement aircraft
8. hazardous

A Notlandung
B gefährlich
C Flugbedingungen
D verbessern
E Ersatzflugzeug
F bequem
G Einstellung
H überhitzen

1	2	3	4	5	6	7	8

FOCUS ON LISTENING → SB p. 103

A13 **5** Listen to the audio and answer the questions.

1. Who is Marcus McCarthy?

____

2. Why is it surprising that Marcus is talking about the aviation industry?

____

____

____

3. What impact does air travel have on the environment?

____

4. What does Marcus say about electric flights?

____

____

____

5. What impact does the weight of a plane have on its fuel efficiency?

____

____

6. What are biofuels?

____

7. Why do only a small number of planes refuel using biofuel?

____

____

____

FOCUS ON SPEAKING → SB p. 103

6 State your opinion about offsetting carbon emissions by completing the following phrases. You may use these sentences in your discussion.

1. Some people see carbon offsetting as ____________________
2. If a company wants to decarbonise air travel, ____________________

   ____
3. Companies in the aviation sector need to ____________________
4. *SAFE AVIATION* could make a greater contribution by ____________________

   ____
5. I think *SAFE AVIATION* should (not) ____________________ because

   ____

FOCUS ON MEDIATION → SB p. 104

7 Mediate the conversation between Jonas, an employee at *SAFE AVIATION*, and Amelia, an English-speaking visitor at the *AirTechSpace* exhibition. Use phrases from the text to help you and use a dictionary if you need to.

Amelia: Hello. Can I ask you some questions about quality management in air and space travel?

You: ____________________

____

Jonas: Ja, bitte.

You: ____________________

Amelia: What is the aim of quality management in this industry in your opinion?

You: ____________________

Jonas: Es hat das Ziel, die Sicherheit, Zuverlässigkeit sowie die Qualität der Produkte sicherzustellen.

You: ____________________

Amelia: I see. So what do manufacturers need to do?

You: ____________________

Jonas: Hersteller müssen eventuelle Sicherheitsrisiken ihrer Produkte kennen und diese auf ein Minimum reduzieren.

You: ____________________

____

Amelia: What are the advantages of a quality management system?

You: ____________________

Jonas: Es gibt mehrere Vorteile. Es hilft Ihnen dabei, frühzeitig Fehler und Schwachstellen zu erkennen und diesen rechtzeitig entgegen zu wirken. Es führt auch zu gesteigerter Produktsicherheit, motivierten Mitarbeitern und zufriedeneren Kunden.

You: ____________________

____

____

TASK 2 | Setting up a product display → SB p. 105

A14 **8** Listen to the audio and complete the advice about how to set up a compressor fan.

Thanks for your voicemail and ______________________ setting up the compressor fan. ______________ the blades are not rotating properly. ________________________ but on the demo version, there's a safety catch to stop the blades moving too freely and accidentally getting damaged, ______________________. ______________ reach underneath the motor to disable this safety catch ____________________. ____________________ the electric motor which rotates the blades for the demo is turned on. ______________________________ and we can arrange a video call so I can see what's happening.

9 Complete the word web with words and phrases you can use to talk about air travel.

Air travel

Passenger safety

____

The impact of technology

____

Making air travel greener

____

Quality management

____

SCENARIO B

UNDERSTANDING THE SCENARIO → SB pp. 106–107

1 Match the following halves of the sentences.

1. I own …
2. My wife and I live …
3. The loft is currently …
4. The original building is …
5. When I'm up there, …
6. Please can you offer me …
7. What would be …

A … on the ground floor.
B … from the 1960s.
C … some advice?
D … a large two-storey house.
E … the next steps?
F … just used for storage.
G … I have to crouch down in places.

1	2	3	4	5	6	7

TASK 1 | Responding to a customer enquiry → SB pp. 107–108

2 Match the phrases from Jeff's email on page 106 with the possible replies. Write the letters in the table.

1. I got your details from a friend of mine for whom you did some work.
2. I've attached a picture to give you a sense of what you'd be working with.
3. What I've got in mind is a studio apartment with its own small kitchen and bathroom.
4. I'm imagining dormer windows might be the order of the day!
5. We want the loft conversion to be as eco-friendly, sustainable and energy-efficient as possible.
6. Please also provide a rough estimation of what the whole job will cost.

A Dormer windows are a great idea for this kind of apartment.
B We are very happy to hear that your friend was pleased with our work.
C Our team will get back to you as soon as possible with a quote.
D The picture you attached is very helpful, thank you.
E Our team has lots of experience with studio apartments.
F Sustainable, energy-efficient building projects are very popular at the moment.

1	2	3	4	5	6

FOCUS ON READING → SB pp. 109 – 110

3 Match the words from the text with their German equivalents.

1. consider
2. thermal conductivity
3. stiff
4. lifespan
5. unwanted
6. temperature sensitive
7. straightforward
8. escalate
9. ventilation
10. nest

A Wärmeleitfähigkeit
B Lebensdauer
C temperaturempfindlich
D berücksichtigen
E Belüftung
F größer werden
G nisten
H starr / fest
I unkompliziert
J unerwünscht

1	2	3	4	5	6	7	8	9	10

4 Read the text and decide if the following statements are true, false or not in the text.

Statement	True	False	Not in text
1. When you are choosing materials, the most important thing to consider is the cost.			
2. Materials with a low K value can hold more heat.			
3. Wood-wool is more cost-effective than hemp quilts.			
4. You need to decide if you want a cold loft or a warm loft.			
5. A warm loft isn't a good idea if you have a loft conversion.			
6. If your loft is already damp, creating a cold loft will make it worse.			

5 Rewrite the sentences below using a gerund for the underlined parts.

1. It's useful to <u>layer different materials</u> in order to get better results.

____

____

2. It is very important to <u>consider what function the loft needs to fulfil</u>.

____

____

3. It will help to avoid rot if you <u>increase the ventilation of the space</u>.

____

____

FOCUS ON VISUALS → SB p. 111

6 Look at diagrams B and C on page 111. Which method would be better for Jeff's loft which he wants to make into a studio apartment? Why? You can use these phrases to help you:

- The loft will be used …
- Jeff's loft has …
- It is important that the loft is …
- The people who live in the studio apartment will want …

FOCUS ON MEDIATION → SB pp. 112 – 113

7 Write down between five and ten keywords in English for each section of the text. You can use a dictionary if you need to.

1. Airtightness for loft conversions
2. Professional fixation
3. Tailored system components

8 Your colleague has made some notes on the text in English, but they have made some mistakes. Underline the wrong words and write the correct words underneath. There is one wrong word or phrase in each sentence.

1. Climate membranes work as vapour barriers in summer.
2. In summer, the pores open because of the cold.
3. The reaction to warm, damp water can cause damage, especially during the construction period.
4. You have to make sure that the climate membrane, alongside the rafters and the foil, creates a cavity-free, closed layer.
5. Tailored system components have to be used to ensure the connection between the vapour barrier and the brickwork is permeable.

FOCUS ON LISTENING → SB p. 113

A15 **9** Listen to the podcast and answer the questions.

1. When did Dave start his business? ______
2. How long did Dave work in construction? ______
3. What two reasons does Dave give for the change in the sort of buildings which large organisations wanted? ______
4. What is the first thing Dave says you should do if you are thinking of starting your own business?
______
______
5. What does Dave give as an example of a service which he outsources? ______
6. What is the dilemma that most people have when they start their own business?
______
7. Why did Dave take on a number of different types of job at the beginning?
______
8. Where is the first caller from? ______

10 Match the words from the podcast to their English definitions. Write your answers in the table below.

1. expertise
2. targets
3. niche
4. launch
5. growing market
6. outsource
7. dilemma
8. complete

A finish
B a market which is getting bigger
C start
D very good knowledge in a particular area
E a difficult choice or decision
F a specialist area
G goals, aims
H ask other people to do particular jobs for you

1	2	3	4	5	6	7	8

FOCUS ON SPEAKING → SB p. 113

11 Decide whether the following arguments are for or against outsourcing. You may use these arguments in your discussion.

Arguments	For	Against
1. It saves time and energy because you don't have to do everything yourself.		
2. It can be more expensive than doing a job yourself.		
3. It can be difficult to make a time plan that suits everyone.		
4. If you outsource a job to someone and they make a mistake, it can damage the reputation of your company.		
5. From the customer's point of view, the quality of the product or service is often better because it is provided by experts.		
6. It gives you more time to focus on other aspects of your company and secure other business opportunities.		

TASK 2 | Discussing options for a customer → SB pp. 114–115

12 Lars is discussing Jeff's loft conversion with Pawel. Match the sentence halves. Who says what? Write L (Lars) or P (Pawel) in the table. For some sentences, the answer could be Lars or Pawel (L / P).

1. I wanted to let you know that …

2. We've had a customer enquiry about …

3. In particular, he's interested in …

4. The customer wants us to consider …

5. If the customer decides to use only sustainable products, …

6. In terms of our current lead times, …

7. Before I can recommend specific products …

8. One thing I'd need to know is …

9. It's important to find out …

10. Let's talk again after …

A … I have spoken to my team.

B … the job will be more expensive.

C … a loft conversion.

D … how old the building is.

E … making the loft conversion eco-friendly.

F … we have a new job that we'd like to work on with you.

G … I need to know more about the building.

H … more about the insulation in the loft.

I … using sustainable materials.

J … we could have the job fully completed by September.

	1	2	3	4	5	6	7	8	9	10
Who?										

SCENARIO C

UNDERSTANDING THE SCENARIO → SB pp. 116 – 117

1 Read the two emails and answer the questions.

1. Where is the work of Cem's team getting noticed?

2. Who would Jason like them to present to?

3. Which language would Jason like to use for the presentation?

4. When are Cem and Jason both available?

5. What examples does Jason give of digital trends in manufacturing?

6. What did Emily find interesting about Cem's Q&A interview in the newsletter?

7. When would Emily like them to give the presentation?

8. Who should Jason contact to find a convenient time?

2 Write Cem's reply to Jason's email. Use these ideas to structure your email:

- Greeting and small talk
- How Cem feels about Emily's email
- How Cem feels about the presentation
- Some of Cem's ideas about what to talk about in the presentation
- The meeting on Thursday afternoon

FOCUS ON READING → SB pp. 119 – 121

3 Summarise the benefits of a connected worker approach. Write one or two sentences for each point.

1. Higher-quality data

2. Simpler data collection

3. Improved worker safety

4. Better communication

5. Better employee engagement

6. Easier hiring

7. Boosted efficiency

FOCUS ON LISTENING → SB p. 121

A16 **4** Listen to the podcast and complete the following assignments.

1. Explain the changes Fatima's company has introduced.

____

____

____

____

2. Explain what the software does.

____

____

____

____

3. Explain what happened as the company continued to introduce more software packages.

____

____

4. Give two benefits that Fatima has noticed since they introduced the connected worker platform. Write two sentences for each benefit.

- ____

  ____

  ____

- ____

  ____

  ____

  ____

5. Give two challenges that the company encountered.

- ____
- ____

  ____

  ____

FOCUS ON MEDIATION → SB pp. 121–122

5 Match the German words with their English equivalents.

1. beinhalten
2. Überblick
3. Wartung
4. Abfall
5. Herstellungskosten
6. vergleichen
7. übersehen
8. Überstunden

A overlook
B include
C production costs
D waste
E overtime
F maintenance
G overview
H compare

1	2	3	4
5	**6**	**7**	**8**

FOCUS ON WRITING → SB pp. 122–123

6 Complete the following sentences with your own opinions.

1. In my opinion, introducing more technology into the workplace is …

2. The main benefit of using more software in the workplace is …

3. I think one problem with using a lot of software in the workplace is …

4. For workers, the most important thing is that …

5. I would like to work somewhere …

FOCUS ON VISUALS → SB p. 123

7 Without looking at the diagram on page 123, put the stages of the Kaizen cycle into the correct order.

A Assess results and determine level of success
B Complete the cycle again regularly
C Compile list of issues, questions and concerns
D Try out the idea
E Select one of the ideas suggested
F Ask for ideas
G Decide whether to implement the idea in the long term
H Ask staff to take part in ongoing improvement process

1	2	3	4	5	6	7	8

TASK 2 | Presenting a proposal → SB pp. 124–125

A17 **8** Listen to Jason's introduction and complete the sentences.

1. Thank you very much for ______________________ for us to speak to you today.
2. My German is ____________________ so I hope you'll forgive me for speaking to you today in English.
3. In a moment, Cem is going to tell you more about ____________________________ he has been researching in view of its potential for implementation at *FlexiDeckel*.
4. ____________________________, I said I wanted to look at how technology can be used to transform what we do here, especially in relation to our production facilities.
5. These benefits and more could be contained within ____________________________ called the connected worker platform.
6. At this point, I would like to ____________________ Cem to tell us more about these areas.

9 After the presentation, members of the Senior Management Team have some questions for Cem. Match their questions with Cem's answers.

1. In your opinion, what is the biggest benefit of connected worker platforms?
2. Do you think there would be disadvantages if we didn't introduce a connected worker platform?
3. Who do you think will benefit most from this technology?
4. Do you think all workplaces will use connected worker platforms in the future?
5. Would we start to see results immediately?
6. Where can we find more information about the ideas you spoke about today?

A Yes, I think we could fall behind our competitors if we don't start using this technology.

B I will send out an email later today with information about how to find out more.

C It's important to have realistic expectations, as the staff need to learn how to use the platform before we start to see results.

D I think everyone will benefit from the platform in different ways, and it will help us all to do our jobs better.

E For me, the best thing about them is that they improve communication so that employees can be more efficient and fulfil their potential.

F I think that connected worker platforms will become very common in the future, and most large companies will probably use them.

1	2	3	4	5	6

EXAM PRACTICE

Teil 1 Hörverstehen → SB p. 128

A18 1 Listen to the audio and select the correct answer for each question or statement below.

1. Paul tests the marketability of a product by ...
   - A ☐ how people respond.
   - B ☐ how many products he sells.
   - C ☐ asking his colleagues what they think.
2. When did Paul design his first invention?
   - A ☐ 1995
   - B ☐ 1997
   - C ☐ 1999
3. How many products has *FastCap* developed since then?
   - A ☐ Over 180
   - B ☐ Over 800
   - C ☐ Over 850
4. Paul is a ...
   - A ☐ builder.
   - B ☐ designer.
   - C ☐ carpenter.
5. Paul invented his first product when he was ...
   - A ☐ frustrated with a simple problem he was having.
   - B ☐ speaking to a customer.
   - C ☐ experimenting in his shop.
6. What does Paul say about creativity?
   - A ☐ There are only some people who are creative enough to invent their own products.
   - B ☐ It is not something which is unique to him or other sucessful inventors.
   - C ☐ Creativity is not the most important skill to have when you are an inventor.
7. Paul says that most people don't know how to ...
   - A ☐ make cabinets.
   - B ☐ start their own business.
   - C ☐ develop products.
8. Where does *FastCap* get a lot of new ideas from?
   - A ☐ Industry experts
   - B ☐ Customers
   - C ☐ Everyday experience

Teil 2 Schriftliche Rezeption → SB pp. 128–129

2 Match the words and phrases from the text with their German equivalents.

1. resilience
2. willingness
3. commonality
4. setback
5. daily
6. adapt
7. shy away from
8. interrupt
9. deepen
10. knowledgeable

A sich anpassen
B Bereitschaft
C Unverwüstlichkeit
D sachkundig
E täglich
F Rückschlag
G Gemeinsamkeit
H vertiefen
I scheuen
J unterbrechen

1	2	3	4	5	6	7	8	9	10

3 Match the problems with the entrepreneurial skills you would need to solve them.

1. Someone in your team is finding their work very difficult and is worried that they won't finish a job on time.	A Resilience
2. You want to make a new website to advertise your business.	B Problem-Solving
3. You are working very hard on a project but you cannot see any results yet.	C Creativity
4. There is some new software which you think would be useful for your business if you took part in some seminars to learn how it works.	D Active Listening and Empathy
5. You have started a job, but it has new challenges you have not experienced before.	E Willingness to Learn and Grow

1	2	3	4	5

Teil 3 Schriftliche Produktion → SB p. 130

4 Write about which entrepreneurial skills you have and which you think you could improve. Give examples of when you have used each of these skills. What kinds of jobs are most suitable for your skills?

Teil 4 Mediation → SB pp. 130–131

5 Read the text and answer the questions in English.

1. What is it important to remember if you have a good idea for a business?
2. What is a big mistake that people often make when they have a business idea?
3. What can you do to make sure you have good enough business knowledge before you start?
4. What do you need to understand about your target market?
5. What do you also need to understand?
6. What is every company based on?
7. What do lots of people hope for when they create a business?
8. What should you do to avoid common financial mistakes when you set up a business?

Teil 5 Rollenbasierte Stellungnahme → SB p. 131

6 Collect words and phrases you can use to discuss being a successful entrepreneur.

4 BUSINESS CORRESPONDENCE
Documenting Processes

COMPARING OFFERS → SB p. 133

1 Look at the different steps when ordering a pizza and match the correct phrase from the word bank to each step.

to carry out an order | to make an enquiry | to submit a request | to make a complaint | to provide payment details | to place an order | to provide confirmation

Situation	Phrase
1. A customer calls *Hot 2 Go* pizza to ask if they offer gluten-free pizzas.	______________
2. After *Hot 2 Go* says gluten-free pizzas are an option on the website, the customer goes online to select the pizzas they want.	______________
3. The customer finds the dietary requirement box and ticks the "gluten-free" option as an additional requirement.	______________
4. After the customer has selected their pizzas and delivery time, they have to enter their card details.	______________
5. Following this, the customer receives an email which says that their order has been accepted.	______________
6. Once the pizzas are ready, *Hot 2 Go* sends their delivery driver out to the customer's address.	______________
7. The customer receives the pizzas, but they seem to be the wrong size so they call *Hot 2 Go* again to express their frustration.	______________

ORDERING → SB p. 133

2 Complete the missing parts of the FAQ section from a business website by writing suitable questions for the answers. The first one has been done for you.

Frequently Asked Questions

1. *When will my order be shipped*?
All orders will be shipped within 1–2 days of receipt of your order.

2. ______________________________?
You can make a claim if you follow this link to our claims page.

3. ______________________________?
You may have got a payment reminder because we have not yet received payment.

4. ______________________________?
You can download a copy of your invoice on your account page.

5. ______________________________?
Unwanted items can be returned by post to the address on our homepage.

6. ______________________________?
We may have cancelled your order due to unusual activity on your account. Please contact us if you have any concerns.

3 Complete the sentences with the correct words from the word bank.

availability | lead time | duties and taxes | supply chain | fair trade | eco-friendliness | reliability | terms and conditions | evaluate | suppliers | order

1. Due to ______________________ issues, the lubricant industry often has to find alternative ____________________ to secure the work process.
2. A long ____________________ means that it takes a long time from placing an _________________ to the final delivery of a product.
3. When looking for a manufacturer, you should not just ___________________ the ____________________ of the goods but also the ____________________ of your business partner, i.e. if they work responsibly.
4. We have attached our ______________________________ to this email for further information.
5. Shipments which cross international borders are subject to __________________________.
6. More and more companies are putting an emphasis on ____________________ and _________________________, in other words sustainability.

4 When placing an order, what detailed information would you expect in each of these categories? Think about orders you or your company have already placed.

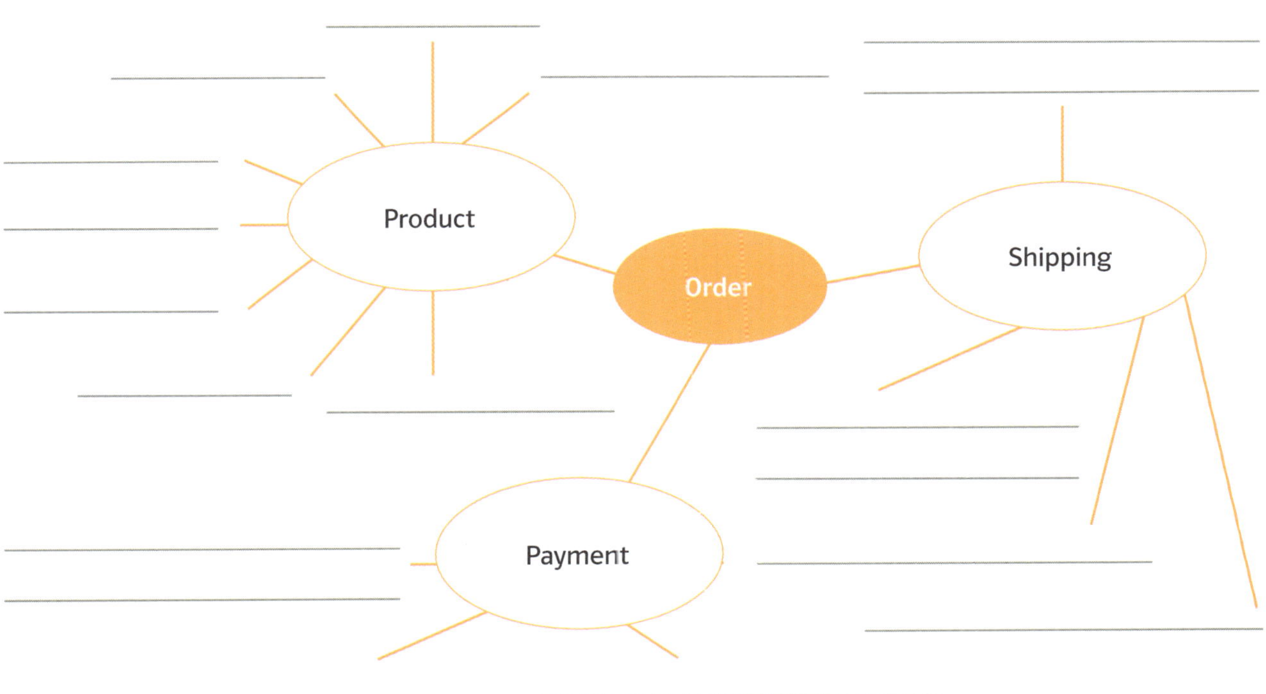

SCENARIO A

UNDERSTANDING THE SCENARIO → SB pp. 134–135

1 Match the verbs with the nouns to form collocations.

1. put	A a full service package
2. request	B over the negotiations
3. take	C fairness
4. attach	D unpleasant surprises
5. add	E points
6. avoid	F a portfolio
7. demonstrate	G on display
8. ensure	H a checklist

2 Complete the table to compare the two different heat pumps more easily. Then retell the information with the help of these keywords.

Information on ...	Quick-a-Heat™ air-source heat pump	CarbonNeutral™ 744 air-source heat pump
Application		
Design		
Costs		
Maintenance		
Performance		
Noise		
Energy efficiency		
Speed of compressor		

3 Choose the correct words from the word bank to match the definitions below.

vent | condenser | compressor | brine | insulation | data sheet | residential application | duct | average | measurement

1. material to reduce the transfer of heat, sound or electricity ____________
2. channel used to transport air ____________
3. solution of salt in water ____________
4. document with detailed information about a product ____________
5. the middle value ____________
6. to compress gas or vapour into a liquid ____________
7. giving the length, time, temperature, etc. ____________
8. opening which air can flow through into a room or building ____________
9. device to increase the pressure of gas or air by reducing its volume ____________
10. used for living in a flat, house or building ____________

TASK 1 | Enquiring with a company about a collaboration → SB pp. 136–137

4 Find the correct number for the different parts of a business email.

reason for writing	☐	information about own company	☐
call to action	☐	subject line	☐
salutation	☐	request for material	☐
polite closing phrase	☐	business proposal	☐
complimentary close	☐	reference to source of information	☐

Enquiry about heat pumps (1)

Dear Sir or Madam, (2)

We refer to your website where you have presented different types of heat pumps. (3) As a consultancy company, we are interested in presenting your products at the *K&K Energy* Exhibition Hub in Essen, Germany. (4)

Our company focusses on sustainable energy solutions. As a partner of different firms, we regularly display innovative technologies at our headquarters here in Essen. (5)

We believe that your products would fit into our range of work perfectly and that a partnership could be mutually beneficial. (6)

If this sounds interesting, we would be most grateful if you could send us specifics on your products and related technical details. (7)

If our proposal is of interest, we could set up a telephone call to discuss a possible partnership in more detail. (8)

We look forward to your reply. (9)

Yours faithfully, (10)

...

5 Look at the list of dos and don'ts when dealing with a supplier successfully and mark the correct columns.

Do	Don't	
		... assess how reliable the supplier is.
		... underestimate your supplier in negotiations.
		... communicate on intentions and requests of both sides.
		... rush to close a deal. Build long-term relations instead.
		... overlook problems in the service of the supplier.
		... select the potential supplier for the price only.
		... address possible problems right away.

FOCUS ON VISUALS → SB pp. 138–139

6 Use the correct words from the visuals to complete the text.

The heat pump system consists of a compressor, indoor and outdoor ________________, a reversing ________________ as well as an expansion device. There are ________________ attached to the coils. A ________________ called refrigerant flows through these parts in a closed cycle. In order to heat the inside, the ______________________ coming from the outdoor coil absorbs heat from the air and boils it to ________________. The indoor coil releases this heat from the refrigerant as it returns to a ________________ state.

With the reversing valve, which is located above the ______________________, the direction of the refrigerant flow can be changed for cooling or defrosting the outdoor coil in winter. When the liquid refigerant enters the ___________________________ the pressure is reduced and the ___________________ is lowered.

7 Rewrite the following sentences in the passive.

1. The producer displays the heating and cooling efficiency performance on the pump.

   ____

2. The fan beside the coil absorbs the air continuously.

   ____

3. You should select a heat pump with a lower outdoor noise rating.

   ____

4. You must protect the units located outdoors from frost.

   ____

5. Technicians check the refrigeration systems at installation.

   ____

FOCUS ON READING → SB pp. 139–141

8 Decide if the following activities concerning heat pumps should be carried out by the user or a technician.

	User	Technician
inspect parts for tightness and wear		
change filters		
clean and tighten connections of the electrical terminal		
clean outdoor coils		
lubricate motors		
remove unnecessary things around the outdoor unit		
diagnose leakage		
clean the grills		
call the technician service regularly		
verify correct thermostat operation		
straighten the fins of the registers if necessary		

9 You have noticed a decrease in the system performance of the heat pump that has recently been installed in your house. Write down tips on what you could do yourself before calling a technician.

10 Use the words and phrases to write sentences comparing underfloor heating (UFH) systems with heating by radiators. You should also add any necessary words.

1. underfloor heating – eco-friendly – using radiators – as – these – energy-efficient

____

____

2. large surface area – use – low – water temperatures – radiators

____

3. installation costs – underfloor heatings – high – but – cheap – in the long run

____

____

4. with UFH – heat – radiate – evenly – across the whole space – with radiators

____

FOCUS ON MEDIATION → SB pp. 142–143

11 Translate the following phrases into English.

1. mit Energie versorgen ______________
2. Solaranlagen installieren ______________
3. Energie erzeugen/generieren ______________
4. das Gasnetz anzapfen ______________
5. seinen eigenen Bedarf decken ______________
6. auf Erdgas umsteigen ______________
7. in die eigene Heizung einbinden ______________
8. sich selbst mit Energie versorgen ______________
9. auf eigene Energiequelle verlassen ______________

12 List the arguments for or against an energy autarchy from the text in English.

For	Against
• ______________	• ______________
• ______________	• ______________
• ______________	• ______________
• ______________	• ______________
• ______________	• ______________
	• ______________

TASK 2 | Following up on an order → SB pp. 144–145

13 Write the English equivalents for the following phrases.

1. Auftragsempfangsbestätigung ______________________
2. vor Ort installieren ______________________
3. aktuelle Lieferzeit ______________________
4. umgehend, frühestmöglich ______________________
5. den Auftrag stornieren ______________________
6. den Preis reduzieren ______________________
7. Vorschläge zur Lösung des Problems ______________________
8. die Installationszeit einschätzen ______________________
9. zögern, jdn. zu kontaktieren ______________________

14 Rewrite the sentences using more formal language.

1. We do not deliver these products at the moment.
____
2. We want to have your answer quickly.
____
3. We enclose brochures.
____
4. We cannot offer you these products anymore.
____
5. We cannot give you a discount.
____
6. Can you send us some sales material?
____

SCENARIO B

UNDERSTANDING THE SCENARIO → SB pp. 146–148

1 Match the words with their definitions.

1. warranty claim
2. service elevator
3. wear on ropes
4. low-maintenance solution
5. feasible
6. heavy-duty job
7. to repurpose

A physically hard work
B damage or degradation of cables
C a lift to transport larger goods or materials
D to give a new function to a product
E a minimum amount of repair and upkeep is necessary
F a request for repair or replacement of a defective product
G practical, can be put into practice

2 Match the following halves of the sentences.

1. A geared system requires the wheel …
2. The motor of a gearless system is mounted …
3. The motors are driven by magnetic force …
4. Inside the magnetic tube of the brushed motor there is a rotor …
5. The brushes contact the commutator …
6. Brushless motors have permanent magnets on the rod (rotator) …
7. Brushless motors rely on electronic devices for their operation, the Hall sensors and the control circuit, …

A … which can be expensive.
B … which is an electromagnet.
C … on top of the elevator cabin.
D … which arises when magnetic fields attract and repel each other.
E … that carries the steel rope called a sheave.
F … that are surrounded by electromagnets fixed to the housing (stator).
G … and allow for the flow of electric current to the copper coils.

1	2	3	4	5	6	7

TASK 1 | Finding and contacting a supplier → SB pp. 148 – 149

3 Translate the following telephone phrases into English.

German	English
Hier ist … am Apparat.	
Ich werde Sie zu ihm durchstellen.	
Bitte bleiben Sie am Apparat.	
Ich werde es Ihnen gleich schicken, während wir noch telefonieren.	
Sie sollten es hoffentlich in nur einer Sekunde haben.	
Ja, die Mail ist gerade angekommen.	
Zögern Sie nicht, mich zu kontaktieren.	
Danke, dass Sie angerufen haben.	

FOCUS ON READING → SB pp. 150 – 151

4 Many prefixes are used for technical terms. Find more examples from the technical field.

Prefix	Meaning	Examples
mono-	single	monorail,
gyro-	circle	gyroscope,
inter-	between	
poly-	many	
sub-	under	
tele-	remote	
dys- / mal-	mis-, bad	
anti- / counter-	against	
auto-	self-	
iso-	same	
il-, im-, in-, ir-	opposite	

FOCUS ON VISUALS → SB p. 152

5 Decide if the following arguments are advantages or disadvantages of hydraulic systems.

	Advantage	Disadvantage
long service life		
possible leakage		
simple operation		
high noise level		
powerful		
harmful hydraulic fluids		
reverse direction possible		
intensive maintenance		
being economical		
regular lubrication necessary		
safe in certain environments (e.g. in chemical plants)		
constant and big force		
expensive price		

TASK 2 | Writing an order to a supplier → SB p. 155

6 Match the nouns from the word bank to the verbs. Multiple combinations are possible.

the order | the goods | a trial order | payment | a form | insurance | terms of payment | the consignment | the quotation

Verb	Noun
to confirm	
to place	
to ship	
to acknowledge	
to insure	
to receive	
to arrange	
to make	
to fill in	

SCENARIO C

UNDERSTANDING THE SCENARIO → SB pp. 156–157

1 Complete the table on materials used in homes.

	Properties	Possible disadvantages	Applications in homes
concrete			
wood/ timber			
steel			
plastic			
stone			
glass			
brick			
carbon fibre			

2 Find examples of tools and materials that the following craftsmen work with in housing projects.

Plumber: ______________________________

Carpenter: ______________________________

Electrician: ______________________________

Tiler: ______________________________

TASK 1 | Discussing components of an offer → SB p. 158

3 The following aspects must be taken into consideration when writing an offer for a new renovation project. Write a heading for each one.

______________: All necessary materials must be included, and their cost accurately estimated.

______________: We must know how many workers we will need.

______________: What specific tasks will we have and which work will not be included?

______________: We must be aware of how long it will take, including for necessary permits and inspections, and we must know when to complete certain stages.

______________: Something could happen, for example somebody might be hurt at work, equipment might be stolen, or something in the house might get broken unintentionally.

______________: There might be payment in advance or a specific payment schedule, but also penalties if we finish our work late.

FOCUS ON READING → SB pp. 159 – 161

4 Complete the following table with words from the same word family.

Noun	Verb	Adjective
contaminant / contamination		
hazard		
		sustainable
		beneficial
perception		
		preferred
occupant /	to occupy	
	to consider	
	to inflame	

5 Read the sentences and decide which word fits better, the adjective or the adverb.

We must be aware that materials used indoors can affect us **mental** | **mentally** and **physical** | **physically**. For example, mould and allergens can **severe** | **severely** damage our health. **Unexpected** | **Unexpectedly** hazards can come from building materials, such as volatile organic compounds which release **harmful** | **harmfully** fumes into the air.

In the case of your **expensive** | **expensively** carpet, it should be removed **immeadiate** | **immediately** when it releases **extreme** | **extremely** high levels of formaldehyde. **Solid** | **Solidly** surface flooring, in contrast, can be cleaned **easy** | **easily** and **normal** | **normally** does not emit **dangerous** | **dangerously** substances. **Similar** | **Similarly** to wood, bamboo can be used as an alternative in the building industry. Other **natural** | **naturally** materials such as wool and cellulose can also be handled **safe** | **safely** to avoid health risks. Another **sustainable** | **sustainably** solution to all these materials is recycled and repurposed materials which **dramatic** | **dramatically** reduce waste in the first place.

6 Choose the correct options to complete the sentences according to the text. There is only one correct option.

1. Indoor air pollution is …
   - A ☐ mainly caused when microorganisms thrive inside homes.
   - B ☐ often difficult to notice.
   - C ☐ less dangerous than outdoor pollution.
2. Different types of pollutants can …
   - A ☐ affect different areas of our well-being.
   - B ☐ exclude each other.
   - C ☐ be ignored.
3. In order to avoid indoor air pollution, we have to use …
   - A ☐ materials that are intentionally made for indoor use.
   - B ☐ natural materials only.
   - C ☐ new building materials.
4. Adhesives should …
   - A ☐ not be used in homes.
   - B ☐ be substituted by hook fastener systems.
   - C ☐ be non-toxic.
5. In contrast to fiberglass, natural materials such as cotton and wool require …
   - A ☐ certifications from the building industry.
   - B ☐ regulated temperatures and airflow.
   - C ☐ relatively litte energy to be produced.

FOCUS ON LISTENING → SB, p. 161

7 Match the words on the left and right to form collocations that describe handling insulating spray foam.

squash | release | expand | trap | soak up | dampen | conduct | lose | reapply | pose | mishandle | regain	the sound | insulants | effectiveness | water | a health hazard | air | a sponge | three times | water | the foam | the sound | its form

____

____

____

A19 **8** Listen to the podcast again. Write down typical signposting phrases used in the presentation.

____

____

____

____

____

FOCUS ON VISUALS → SB p. 162

9 Put the instructions on how to install hardwood floors into the correct order and add the necessary words from the visual.

	You could start with the side of most doorways where you place the planks against the bottom of the ________ or you trim the bottom of the jambs to have the flooring underneath.
	This underlayment needs to be ________ at the seams.
	After that, push this second board with its groove into the ________ of the first board.
	At the corners to the wall, the ________ must be applied as they give a smooth transition from the floor to the wall.
	Painter's tape can be used to hold ________ together until the glue dries.
1	Measure the space where you intend to install the hardwood floor and order the material.
	This process must be repeated until the room is completely covered with the flooring.
	Apply adhesive or ________ to the subfloor.
	Start by laying the first board with the ________ to the wall but put a ________ to the wall.
	The glue should cure for some hours before the ________ and ________ can be removed.
	Squeeze ________ into the end of the groove of the next board.
	After delivery, let the wood acclimate to the room.

FOCUS ON MEDIATION → SB, pp. 162 – 163

10 Match the sentence halves and add the most suitable auxiliary verb from the word bank.

must | might | need to | should | could | are allowed to | might | have to

1. Homeowners who are planning a loft conversion …	A ________________ be observed.
2. Violation of regulations for fire protection and thermal insulation …	B if a new apartment is getting built.
3. A building permit ________________ be required, …	C ________________ be preserved and corresponding materials be used.
4. If owners have the sole right of use for an attic …	D renovation and construction measures more complex and expensive.
5. Monument conservation ________________ make …	E they ________________ decide on its future use.
6. A number of regulations for fire protection and thermal insulation …	F ________________ inform themselves about legal requirements in advance.
7. Parking spaces ________________ be provided …	G ________________ result in a fire.
8. Because of monument conservation regulations, the historic character of an old building …	H especially if there are changes to the roof area.

1	2	3	4	5	6	7	8

TASK 2 | Writing a formal quotation → SB pp. 164–165

11 Choose a heading from the word bank for each group of words.

materials | dimensions | verbs to handle joists | voids | properties | costs

manoeuvre, trim, attach, place, install	
susceptible to fire, sturdy, eco-friendly, cantilevered	
pricey, expensive, cost-intensive, costly	
lumber, old-growth, veneer, wood, middle-plywood, timber, OSB	
cutout, cuts, notches, holes	
length, height, depth, width	

12 Complete the following quotation form with the missing words from the word bank.

Warranty period | delivery | Packing | Unit price | Reference number | Mode of transport | Shipping | Tax | signature | Delivery time | Amount | Item description | discount | Validity of offer | Terms of payment | receipt of order | Bank transfer | terms and conditions

Quotation for lumber joists

To: InsulDach, Dachstraße 23, Köln

____________________: TJ0457

Quotation date: 23 January, 20…

____________________	Quantity	____________ (in Euros)	____________ (in Euros)
Materials		33	6,600.00
lumber joists 50 x 200 x 390mm	200	____________ 19 %	1254.00
		Introductory ____________ 4 %	264.00
____________			300.00
TOTAL			7890.00

____________ inclusive: cellulose-based

____________: 14 days

____________: by lorry

____________: 2 years

____________: 20 February, 20…

____________:

60 % payment made on ____________. 40 % to be paid on ____________.

Payment method: ____________; Sparkasse …, IBAN: …

For further information on our ____________ please see our website: host@kl.eu

Client____________:

Date:

EXAM PRACTICE

Teil 1 Hörverstehen → SB p. 168

A20 **1** Translate the words from the audio into German and add a short definition in English. Then listen and check your answers.

English	German	Definition
communication	____________ ____________	____________ ____________
temperature	____________ ____________	____________ ____________
balanced	____________ ____________	____________ ____________
to adjust	____________ ____________	____________ ____________
wheelchair	____________ ____________	____________ ____________
benefit	____________ ____________	____________ ____________
disabled	____________ ____________	____________ ____________

Teil 2 Schrifliche Rezeption → SB pp. 168–169

2 Put in the correct prepositions.

1. improvement ______ the performance
2. adapt ______ the user
3. base model ______ data
4. walk ______ various conditions
5. compare ______ measurements
6. ______ different speeds
7. ________ a range of conditions
8. wear ______ the waist
9. equal ______ the energy savings
10. result ______ improvements

3 Complete the following advertisement for the new robotic exoskeleton.

Exoskeleton – your new companion

Do you have ______________________ which result in walking difficulties, have to carry ________________ or must ______________ strenuous movements?

Our new exoskeleton personalises ________________ in the real world and it can rapidly ______________ you during normal walking. This revolutionary consumer medical ____________ has already been tested outdoors on ____________________, and on average we increased the walking speed by 9 % and _______________ 17 % less energy!

With our exoskeleton we have created a ______________, ________________ device which is powered by a _________________ worn at the waist. With each step, a motor provides ____________ at the ankle and in this way the user can push off.

With our new exoskeleton it is no longer necessary to collect ______________ data about users' movement or their __________________ which makes expensive lab _______________ or walking on a ______________ redundant.

► For further information you can contact us at _____________________.

4 Connect the following sentences by using relative clauses. Can you also use participles to shorten these relative clauses?

1. Millions of people have conditions. These conditions make everyday movements difficult.

   ____

2. Wearable robotic devices could benefit different people. They are called exoskeletons.

   ____

3. A research team at Stanford University has developed an exoskeleton. This team was led by Dr. Steven Collins.

   ____

   ____

4. The researchers based their model on metabolic data. They had collected this data in a programme before.

   ____

   ____

5. The team tested how well an exoskeleton could adapt to a user. The exoskeleton was based on their model.

   ____

   ____

6. The exoskeleton was powered by a battery pack. It was worn at the waist.

   ____

Teil 3 Schriftliche Kommunikation → SB p. 170

5 Translate the German phrases into English.

1. eine Beschwerde erhalten ______
2. der Fehler passierte, weil … ______
3. die obengenannte Kundennummer ______
4. sich beschweren über … ______
5. über die Garantie abdecken ______
6. sich für Unannehmlichkeiten entschuldigen ______
7. die Angelegenheit in Ordnung bringen ______
8. die fehlerhaften Batterien ersetzen ______
9. zu Ihrer vollsten Zufriedenheit ______

Teil 4 Mediation → SB pp. 170 – 171

6 The following six headlines and sets of words might help you to write your mediation. Draw lines to connect each set of words to a headline.

1 Definition of exoskeletons

2 Hazards to person with wearable exoskeleton

3 Exoskeletons for occupational safety

support, application, serious injuries, competitive sports, physical performance, to relieve

to cause overloads, musculoskeletal disorders, occupational diseases

leaf springs, to tension, accidentally, be pinched, to affect

to restrict, to hinder, to malfunction, defective motor

to simulate in a laboratory, to measure, entire body, to take away the load, to redirect, to reintroduce, critical areas, to stress / be under stress

wearable, framework, distinguish between, to release energy

4 Hazards associated with the use of exoskeletons to other people

5 Functions of exoskeletons

6 Exoskeletons to reduce physical stress?

Teil 5 Rollenbasierte Stellungnahme → SB p. 171

7 Collect words and phrases you can use to discuss the functions and benefits of an exoskeleton.

______

______

______

______

5 INTERNAL AND EXTERNAL COMMUNICATION
Planning and organising

MEANS OF COMMUNICATION → SB p. 173

1 Match the correct means of communication from the word bank with the descriptions.

non-verbal communication | facial expression | verbal communicaton | oral communication
sign language

Description	Means of communication
1. Using the voice to communicate either face-to-face or by telephone	______
2. Expressing feelings e.g. by a smile or frown	______
3. Like spoken language but makes use of the hands and face to convey a message	______
4. Giving implicit messages which aren't necessarily words, especially with gestures	______
5. Conveying opinions, ideas and feelings through conversations, speeches, etc.	______

2 Write down two advantages and two disadvantages for each of the following means of communication. You don't need to use full sentences.

	Advantages	Disadvantages
Telephone	______ ______	______ ______
Face-to-face	______ ______ ______	______ ______ ______
Social media	______ ______	______ ______
Written	______ ______ ______	______ ______ ______
Video call	______ ______ ______	______ ______ ______

COMMUNICATION SKILLS AT WORK → SB p. 173

A21 **3** Listen to the audio and mark the aspects of communication skills in the technological sector that are mentioned for each section.

Communications skills are often…	overvalued		undervalued	
Examples of soft skills	networking		collaborating	
	adapting to situations		presenting	
Communication skills important for developing …	rapport		mutual respect	
	problem-solving		understanding	
	positive relationships		leadership	
Example situations of good communication skills	informing of important changes on a project		conflict resolution	
	having a job interview		finding out how a presentation went	
Examples of non-verbal communication	body language		facial expressions	
	gestures		touch	
	tone of voice		eye contact	
Reasons why listening is important	building relationships		to understand problems	
	helping to prepare answers		learning	
Complex examples of written communication	product manual		installation guide	
	instructions for customers		report for senior management	

INSTRUCTIVE COMMUNICATION → SB p. 173

4 Complete the text about bicycle maintenance and repairs with the words from the word bank. You can use the words more than once.

many | much | more | (a) little | (a) few | less | least

Here are ______________ tips for repairing and maintaining your own bicycle. If there is too ______________ lubricant on the chain, clean it as it might get too sticky. A ______________ bike degreaser might help you, or at ______________ use some dish soap. You can hear ______________ bicycles on the road making a grinding noise. A first step could be to put ______________ lubricant on the chain every ______________ weeks. ______________ air loss in your tyres is normal. But if you have an unexpected flat, the reason could be debris or glass in your tyre. Although patching the tyre costs ______________ money, it is often easier to just exchange it. Adjusting brakes and replacing cables is ______________ work and when you have gained ______________ experience you could do more complex repairs yourself. ______________ toolkits contain wrenches, sockets and screwdrivers. Just try them out!

SCENARIO A

UNDERSTANDING THE SCENARIO → SB pp. 174–175

1 Find the full words for the abbreviations that are used in the car industry.

AWD	______	FWD	______
SUV	______	OBD	______
PHEV	______	TPMS	______
ESC	______	LDAS	______

2 Match each description with one of the abbreviations from Exercise 1.

1. This safety system helps drivers to maintain control of their vehicles in unstable conditions. ______
2. This function assists you with staying in your lane. ______
3. In SUVs, it often comes as standard to have better traction and handling on uneven roads. ______
4. This electronic system provides vehicle self-diagnosis for technicians. ______
5. This system will alert you when tyres are below the necessary air pressure. ______

TASK 1 | Contacting technical support → SB p. 176

3 Look at the list of dos and don'ts when calling technical support and mark the correct columns.

Do	Don't	
		… get emotional about the problem.
		… have necessary reference number or specifications ready.
		… talk fast and / or quietly.
		… be prepared with necessary information before you start the conversation.
		… maintain a friendly voice.
		… share sensitive information as this can pose a security risk.
		… speak in complete sentences when talking to a chatbot.
		… ask for clarification if there is still something you don't understand.

FOCUS ON READING → SB pp. 177 – 179

4 Complete the phrases with the verbs from the word bank.

last | detect | be equipped | avoid | determine | reflect | make | predict | calculate | emit | gather | require

1. ____________ with sensors
2. ____________ information about surroundings
3. ____________ off objects and surfaces
4. ____________ the distance to the object
5. ____________ photons
6. ____________ the shape and size of objects
7. ____________ pedestrians
8. ____________ where the pedestrian will walk
9. ____________ advance notice
10. ____________ a collision
11. ____________ proper decisions
12. ____________ a million miles

5 Number the steps to show how the LIDAR works.

	A huge number of data points are generated.
	The laser light is reflected back towards the LIDAR sensor.
	The sensor emits laser light at multiple angles.
	The sensor processes the resulting calculations and creates a detailed 3D map.
	Then, the sensor calculates the distance to the target object.
	After detecting the reflected light, the LIDAR measures the time of the reflection.
1	A LIDAR sensor emits light waves towards a target object.
	The emitted light hits the target objects and surfaces.

6 Mark which type of remote sensing technology each sentence describes.

	RADAR	LIDAR
1. It uses radio waves to detect and measure distances.		
2. It has a shorter range but higher accuracy.		
3. It can be more easily affected by fog, rain and dust.		
4. It can detect larger objects at a range of many kilometres.		
5. It is generally more expensive due the complex electronics necessary.		
6. It is often used in air traffic control and for military purposes.		
7. It can penetrate through fog and clouds.		
8. It can create 3D maps of the environment.		

7 Write sentences to contrast the following issues of LIDAR and RADAR sensoring. Use one of the phrases from the word bank in each sentence.

in contrast to | however | unlike | whereas | as opposed to

1. Range

___

___

2. Accuracy

___

___

3. Cost

___

4. Weather conditions

___

___

5. Sensitivity

___

___

FOCUS ON MEDIATION → SB pp. 179–180

8 Translate the following phrases into German.

1. legal regulations ___
2. longitudinal and lateral motion ___
3. human intervention ___
4. upon request ___
5. parking space ___
6. liability disclaimer ___

9 Match the verbs on the left with the nouns on the right. Write the phrases below.

recognise | master | monitor | perform | be responsible for | take | handle | define

control | levels | limits | the system | the ride | manoeuvres | journeys | situations

___

___

___

FOCUS ON VISUALS → SB p. 181

10 Put the following safety systems into the correct category.

lane departure warning | seat belts | electronic stability control | crumple zones | braking systems | headrests | forward-collision warning | shoulder belt | adaptive cruise control | blind spot detection | front-crash prevention | ABS | park assistance | air bags | side mirrors | bumper | ESC

Active Safety Systems to prevent an accident before it actually happens	**Passive Safety Systems** to minimise damage and reduce the risk of injury in a crash
__________	__________
__________	__________
__________	__________
__________	__________
__________	__________
__________	__________
__________	__________
__________	__________
__________	__________
__________	__________

TASK 2 | Relaying complex technical information → SB p. 183

A22 **11** Listen to the audio and complete the missing words.

Sensor module

Keeps track of vehicle and road ________________:

- motion of host and target vehicle: speed, ________, ________________
- host vehicle ____________ and ____________
- road parameters: road conditions, tyre-road friction coefficient (obtained by ______________ and / or by analysing the vehicle's ______________ to changes)

Decision module

Can issue an ________________ or decide on ____________________

- "relative distance-based discrimination method": comparing relative distance to ____________ threshold value (____________________, speed, maximum braking ______________)
- "time to collision" calculation: based on vehicle's expected ________________

Actuation module

- enforces emergency brake action
- braking pressure distributed accordingly on ____________________

SCENARIO B

UNDERSTANDING THE SCENARIO → SB pp. 184–185

1 Complete the sentences with the words from the word bank.

fault | defects | error | failure | malfunctions | checks | test | controls | inspection | maintenance

1. The material tester found out that the cause of the material __________________ was corrosion.
2. The ____________________ of an aircraft component can have catastrophic consequences.
3. When the pilot makes a wrong decision, it is referred to as human __________________.
4. After assessing ____________________, it is determined whether the aircraft can still fly.
5. A pilot is taught to understand the operation and typical __________________________ of engines.
6. Airline companies are obliged to follow certain _________________________ plans.
7. Before take-off the pilot does some ____________________ of sensors, lights, tyres, etc.
8. What do all the ____________________ in the cockpit of the aircraft do?
9. In general, _______________________ requirements do not differ in international aviation.
10. The _________________ of the new aircraft was carried out under actual flight conditions.

2 There is one incorrect word in each group. Underline the words and give a reason why each is wrong.

1. wings – fuselage – pylon – pod
   Reason: ____
2. pin – batch – bolt – screw
   Reason: ____
3. crack – fracture – alloy – corrosion
   Reason: ____
4. treatment – thrust – vibration – flutter
   Reason: ____
5. detect – notify – reevaluate – solve
   Reason: ____

3 Match the mechanical properties below with their definitions. Then translate the words into German.

elasticity | hardness | ductility | toughness | malleability | brittleness | tensile strength

Definition	Mechanical property	German translation
absorbing energy without getting broken	______	______
being rigid and resistant to pressure, abrasion, scratching	______	______
the measure to pull something until it is torn or broken	______	______
deform without breaking when subjected to tensile stress	______	______
property when material is worked on and shaped	______	______
ability of breaking of material when exposed to stress	______	______
to return to original shape after being distorted or deformed	______	______

TASK 1 | Getting support with a communications issue → SB p. 186

4 Look at the names of departments on page 186. Choose which department would be responsible for the following tasks.

Tasks	Department
1. They work on developing modifications to prevent a mechanical, electrical or hydraulic issue from occurring in the future.	______
2. They advertise the new model of the aircraft and promote issues like safety, size and speed.	______
3. They coordinate the work of all other departments and ensure that necessary resources are available.	______
4. If an aircraft had defective parts, this department could defend the company against legal claims.	______
5. The staff in this department work to ensure that necessary parts or materials are sourced quickly and efficiently.	______
6. The technicians in this department identify whether the aircraft fulfils all technical standards. They also carry out control measures to prevent technical problems.	______

FOCUS ON LISTENING → SB p. 187

5 Match the words from the podcast with their definitions.

1. crevice corrosion
2. exfoliation
3. solution
4. moisture
5. be exposed to
6. detrimental
7. to penetrate
8. honeycombs

A to seep into a material or surface
B hexagonal cell structures made by bees to store honey
C the corrosion in narrow gaps or spaces between two surfaces
D harmful, damaging because of a chemical reaction
E the presence of water in the air or on surfaces
F corrosion where metal layers become separated
G substance that is dissolved in a solvent
H to come into contact with sth. or be subjected to its influence

1	2	3	4	5	6	7	8

6 Complete the following sentences to explain the issue of corrosion.

1. Mechanical properties which corrosion affects are ______
2. Corrosion can take place on ______
3. When metal is exposed to moisture ______
4. Corrosion can be prevented with ______
______
5. In an aircraft, corrosion can do damage to ______

FOCUS ON READING → SB pp. 187–189

7 Write definitions for the words from the text.

composite (l. 2) ______
______

oven (l. 12) ______
______

properties (l. 14) ______
______

layer (l. 25) ______
______

reinforcement (l. 25) ______
______

microfracture (l. 31) ______
______

8 Complete the text about the advantages of self-healing materials with the words from the word bank.

lifespan | remove | fracture | failure | service | longevity | strength | sustainable | available

Self-healing materials offer numerous advantages, including the ability to repair themselves in place without being removed from ____________________. They extend the ____________________ of structural components, i.e. ____________________, and retain ____________________ and performance characteristics without engineers having to worry about ____________________. This makes self-healing materials more ____________________ than traditional ones. Additionally, self-healing can be repeated at least 100 times. These composites also enhance inherent resistance to ____________________ and use readily ____________________ materials that are relatively inexpensive. With planes, self-healing materials can stop the need for using chemical agents to ____________________ ice from wings.

9 Find the words in the word snake that are related to safety issues when transporting lithium batteries.

flammablefireextinguisheroverheatdefectiveexplosioninjuryaccidentexposeoverheatingdisposalemergency

____

____

FOCUS ON VISUALS → SB p. 190

10 Match the following halves of the sentences.

1. If an aircraft climbs to higher altitudes, …	A … which can lead to passenger dizziness or even confusion.
2. At higher altitudes the air pressure is lower …	B … to ensure the safety of the aircraft.
3. The cabin of an aircraft is pressurised to maintain …	C … which can affect the stability of the aircraft.
4. Pilots must be aware of the altitude and air pressure at all times …	D … pilots might have to change the altitude and adjust the angle of the aircraft.
5. Changes in altitude and air pressure can cause turbulence …	E … a comfortable air pressure and temperature for passengers.
6. In the event of a sudden drop, …	F … and the temperature is colder.
7. When an aircraft climbs or descends rapidly the air pressure changes, …	G … the air pressure outside the plane decreases.

1	2	3	4	5	6	7

FOCUS ON MEDIATION → SB pp. 191–192

11 Write words in English for the following categories.

manufacturing technologies: ______________________________

____

____

____

surfaces: ______________________________

____

regulations: ______________________________

____

materials: ______________________________

____

TASK 2 | Communicating with visitors → SB p. 193

12 Choose the correct word to complete the questions which could be asked at the stand of a trade fair.

Visitor

1. How does your company … itself from your competitors?
   A ☐ differentiate B ☐ divide C ☐ separate D ☐ differ
2. What are the main … of using corrosion-free materials?
   A ☐ uses B ☐ applications C ☐ operations D ☐ ideas
3. Do you have any customer … for your products?
   A ☐ proof B ☐ evidence C ☐ testimonials D ☐ prove
4. What services does your company …?
   A ☐ deliver B ☐ provide C ☐ assess D ☐ excel

Customer

5. What are your … for attending this trade fair?
   A ☐ goals B ☐ ideas C ☐ interests D ☐ recommendations
6. Have you … our presentation on safety standards in aviation?
   A ☐ visited B ☐ been C ☐ attended D ☐ heard
7. Would you like to … business cards to stay in touch?
   A ☐ change B ☐ exchange C ☐ give D ☐ hand out

SCENARIO C

UNDERSTANDING THE SCENARIO → SB pp. 194 – 195

1 Which type of brake would the following applications require?

______________________ are used in industrial machinery such as cranes because they are designed to handle high torque loads.

______________________ are often installed in modern vehicles because of their superior performance.

______________________ are in use for many machine tools such as lathes and milling machines.

______________________ are used for winches to control the movement of heavy loads.

2 Complete the sentences with the verbs in the word bank in the correct form.

slow down | clamp | disperse | hold | dissipate | occur | clamp shut | push | stationary

1. By using friction brakes, you can ______________________ or even stop the moving parts.
2. When the brakes are applied, they ______________________ which helps to ______________________ the object ______________________.
3. Metal brake drums absorb the heat which is then ______________________ into the atmosphere.
4. As the brake drums have a large surface area, heat can quickly be ______________________.
5. When braking, the brake shoes inside the brake drum are ______________________ outwards.
6. In electromagnetic brakes, wear can ______________________ on the faces of the mating surfaces.
7. Rim brakes are typically used on bicycles, and they ______________________ directly on the sides of the wheel rim.

3 Match the following terms for brake operation with their definitions.

1. power dissipation
2. brake torque
3. residue
4. brake fluid
5. response time
6. lever force
7. slip indication

A brake reaction time
B the total available force that a braking system can apply
C the amount of force to the rotors to slow them down
D power that the brake can withstand before failing
E feedback that the braking system does not perform properly
F liquid chemical solution used in hydraulic braking systems
G brake dust that collects on the wheels

1	2	3	4	5	6	7

TASK 1 | Dealing with customer complaints → SB p. 196

4 Put the following words about problems or solutions when amending an order into the correct column.

offer compensation | offer repair | record the complaint | extra costs | wrong quantity | damaged products | offer a discount | investigate the cause | missing products | bad quality | damaged packaging | apologise sincerely | send a replacement | resend the order | slow / late shipment | incomplete order

Problems	Solutions

5 Put the following email of apology to a customer into the correct order.

	As further compensation, we would like to offer you a discount of 10 % on your next order, using code XX10.
	Yours sincerely,
	Firstly, we would like to apologise that our consignment did not meet your requirements.
	Once again, we apologise for any inconvenience this has caused.
	Thank you for your email regarding a faulty delivery of brake pads.
1	Dear Julia,
	The order is expected to be shipped by the end of this week.
	If you have any other questions please reply to this email.
	You will shortly be sent a replacement of the goods.
	Please use this code at the check out when placing your next order.
	After checking the problem, we found an error in our order fulfilment system.

FOCUS ON READING → SB pp. 197 – 198

6 Complete the following table with words from the same word family.

Noun	Verb	Adjective
		redundant
accumulation		
	to prevent	
		prior
	to verify	
		acceptable
	to ascertain	
tightness		
		necessary

7 Read the text and decide whether the statements are true or false.

Statement	True	False
1. Modern passenger elevators only need one braking system.		
2. Brakes are also necessary when the elevator is moving properly.		
3. Using more lubricants than specified is safer and ensures smooth operation.		
4. Brake discs in elevators are applied during the movement of the car.		
5. When brake discs are not maintained regularly they become thinner.		
6. Spare parts are necessary when the gap is more than 0.04 inches.		
7. The only tools needed to adjust brakes are feeler gauges and wrenches.		

FOCUS ON WRITING → SB p. 199

8 Put the tasks a technician must complete when inspecting an elevator into the correct order.

	Ride the elevator again and open and close doors.
	Verify that doors open and close properly on all levels.
	Carry out service work.
	Perform a tool audit of the equipment of the elevator.
1	Inform the tenants in the building that maintenance work is scheduled.
	Complete the maintenance template and inform if any repairs must be done.
	Shut down all electrical circuits during the service work.
	Ride the elevator to note any noise, vibration or unusual movement.

FOCUS ON LISTENING → SB p. 199

A23 **9** Listen to the audio and mark the safety equipment, tools and spare parts that are mentioned.

Safety equipment		Tools		Spare parts	
safety mask		pliers		pulleys	
rubber-insulated mats		hammer		cables	
gloves		wrenches		screws	
goggles		spanners		fasteners	
earplugs		punches		nuts	
safety helmet		duct tape		washers	
rubber boots		film tape		bolts	
protection harness		tape measure		brake discs	
ladder		shears		brake pad linings	

FOCUS ON VISUALS → SB p. 200

10 Write the correct term for each of the tools below.

1. It is a cutting tool to work on wood, stone or metal. ____________________

2. It is used to cut through steel or other metals. ____________________

3. This sharp utility knife is used for cutting, stripping wire, etc. ____________________

4. Nuts and bolts must must be fastened or loosened. ____________________

5. You seal something or patch holes with it. ____________________

6. Solder is heated and workpieces are then joined. ____________________

7. It determines if there is an inclination between two spots. ____________________

8. An object can be gripped and it has handles, a pivot and jaws. ____________________

1
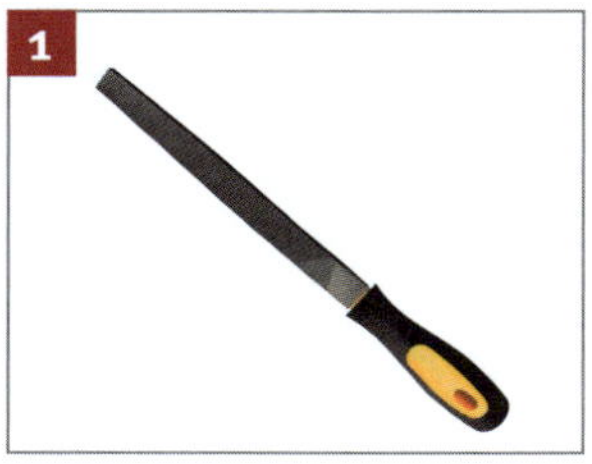

2

3

4
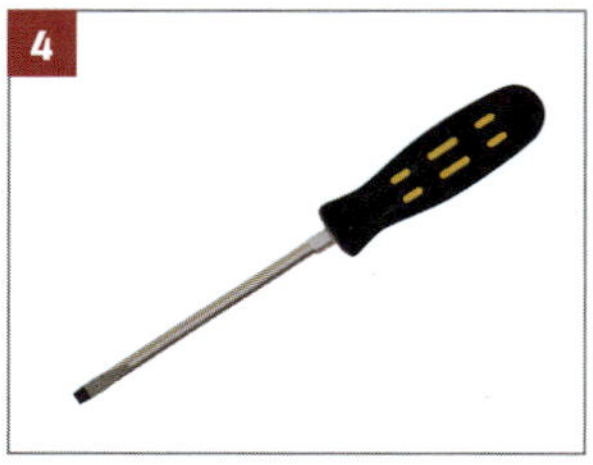

5

6

7

8

FOCUS ON MEDIATION → SB pp. 201 – 202

11 Match the following English words to the category as mentioned in the mediation text.

1 Legally mandated inspections

2 Possible cyberattacks because of IoT

encrypted communication, high-quality authentication, approach to cybersecurity

occupational safety, social security, social accident insurance

dangerous / significant / minor defects

IoT-connected technology, communication systems, controls

approved monitoring agency, building management, elevator operator

shut down, repair on the spot

harm, fatalities

visible, indicate, pass the date

access to critical data, digital attacks

3 Central collection of accidents

4 Inspection sticker

1. Legally mandated inspections:

____

____

____

2. Possible cyberattacks because of IoT:

____

____

____

3. Central collection of accidents:

____

____

____

4. Inspection sticker:

____

____

____

EXAM PRACTICE

Teil 1 Hörverstehen → SB p. 206

A24 🔈 **1** Match the forms to the corresponding nouns to form collocations used in the audio. Then listen to the podcast and check your answers.

1. to power	A sb's life
2. to touch	B an answer
3. to take	C a bus / car
4. to take	D as a (heat) source
5. to provide	E the process
6. to give	F heat
7. to use	G a way
8. to have	H the oxygen out

Teil 2 Schriftliche Rezeption → SB pp. 206 – 207

2 Complete the following word web with information from the text.

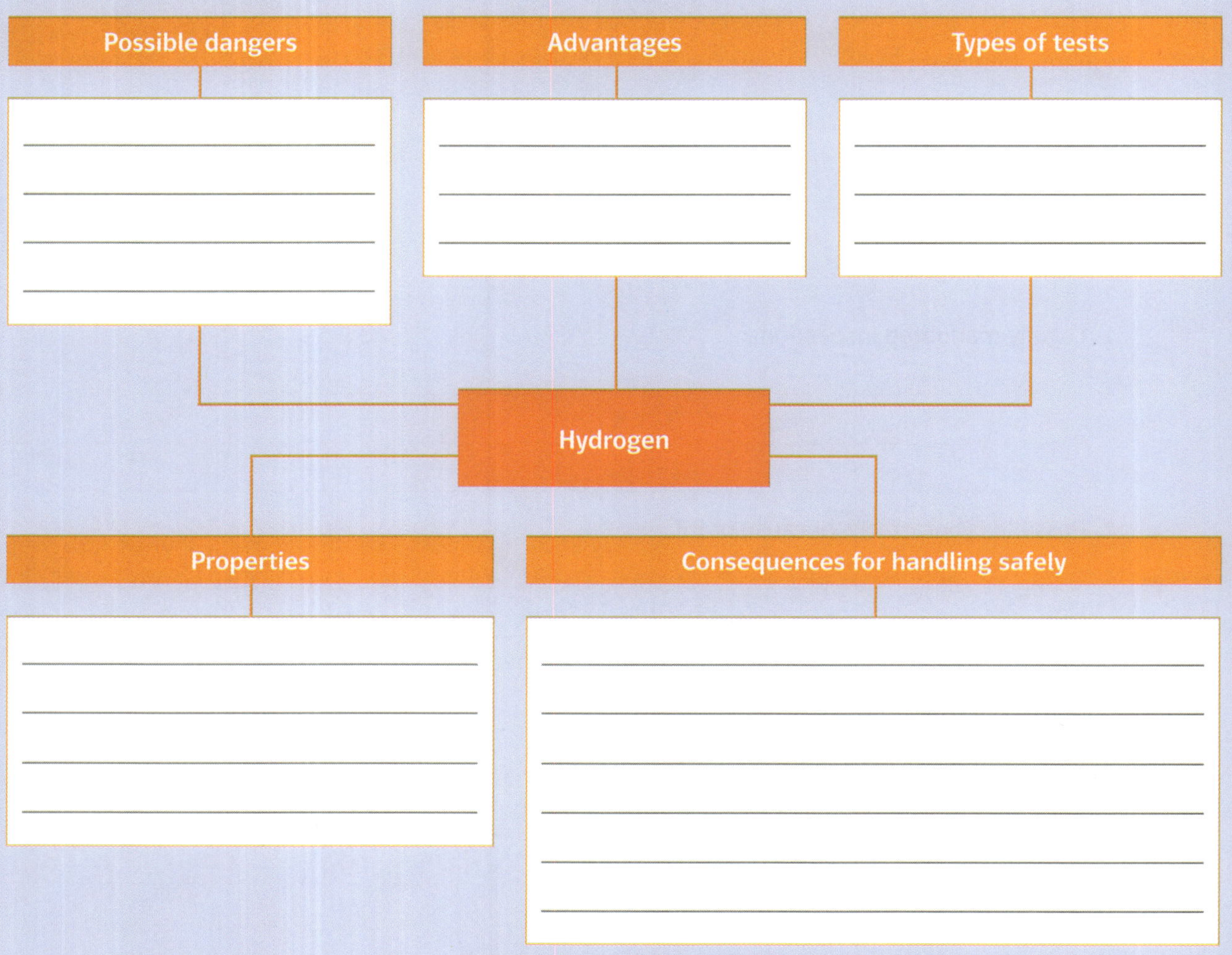

Teil 3 Schriftliche Produktion → SB p. 207

3 Complete the email with the necessary information.

To: smith@dutchutilities.eu, miller@dutchutilities.eu, johns@dutchutilities.eu …
From: xxx@dutchutilities.eu
Subject: ____________________

Dear team members,

I am inviting you to ____________________. The main purpose of the meeting is to discuss ____________________. I would also like to talk about ____________________. In our meeting, we will evaluate whether ____________________. I have attached ____________________. Please ensure that you are well informed about ____________________.

If you have any questions beforehand, ____________________. Please respond to this email by ____________________.

Many thanks,

Teil 4 Mediation → SB pp. 208 – 209

4 At a forum of international experts on hydrogen, you are asked questions about Germany's approach to this issue. Find the answers in the text, then act out the dialogue with a partner.

A: I have heard of the German Hydrogen Research Network. What do they work on?

B: ____________________

A: I have read something about Germany's energy transition. Does hydrogen play a part there as well?

B: ____________________

A: Can you give me some examples of sectors and industries in which hydrogen could be important?

B: ____________________

A: How is the German Hydrogen Research Network funded?

B: ____________________

A: Could you name some organisations and other players that are working in the Hydrogen Research Network?

B: ____________________

A: How can the different players from various research disciplines and practice work together within the Hydrogen Research Network?

B: ____________________

A: What do the members of the network focus on?

B: ____

____

A: I have heard that the network is divided into clusters. What are they?

B: ____

____

A: Thank you for the information.

Teil 5 Rollenbasierte Stellungnahme → SB p. 209

5 Underline any words which you associate positively or negatively with the fact that a company gets tax deductions and / or subsidies. These words might help you to discuss this topic later on.

incentives | burden | behaviour

growth | in/efficiency | competitive | lobby

competition | fiscal impact | risky

taxpayer | boost | opportunity | profits

encourage | protection | support

free market | corrupt/ion | overconsumption | beneficiary

overproduction | demand and supply | positive / negative externalities

6 CONFLICT MANAGEMENT
Dealing with issues at work

TALKING ABOUT CONFLICTS → SB p. 211

1 Complete the crossword puzzle with words that have something to do with conflict situations.

Down:

1. to prevent sb from thinking clearly
2. to make sb feel uncomfortable or angry
3. the belief that sth is going to happen
6. to give up on one's original wishes in order to achieve a solution
8. a conversation in which people strongly disagree with each other

Across:

4. the result of different parties coming to the same opinion
5. to trigger sb to have a certain reaction
7. to try hard under difficult circumstances
9. an expression of dissatisfaction with sb / sth
10. to recommend sth in order to help sb
11. an angry disagreement with sb
12. to say sth impolite in order to offend sb
13. a problem caused to sb
14. a way to deal with a specific problem

CONFLICTS AT WORK → SB p. 211

2 What problems might arise in the following types of relationships at work? Complete the word webs with relevant ideas.

Between employees and management

dissatisfied

Among colleagues

uncommunicative

DESCRIBING WAYS TO SOLVE CONFLICTS AT WORK → SB p. 211

3 List some ideas for solving a problem with somebody you have conflicts with.

____

____

____

____

____

____

____

SOLUTIONS FOR CONFLICTS AT WORK → SB p. 211

A25 **4** Listen to the audio and complete the table with the four problems at work and and the solutions.

	Problems	Solutions
1		
2		
3		
4		

SCENARIO A

UNDERSTANDING THE SCENARIO → SB pp. 212–213

1 Find the English translations for the following phrases in the email.

English	German
Ich bin darüber verärgert, dass Sie diese Entscheidung gemacht haben, ohne mich vorher zu konsultieren.	______ ______
Es ist nicht akzeptabel, nicht (zu tun) …	______
Ich bin mir sicher, dass Sie nicht respektlos sein wollten.	______ ______
… würde für uns ein großes Problem darstellen.	______
Es würde auch Probleme verursachen.	______
Daher kann ich das nicht unterzeichnen.	______
Ich bitte Sie, eine andere Lösung zu finden.	______
unter unnötigen Stress zu setzen	______
Sie müssen eine bessere Lösung finden.	______

2 Complete the *if*-clauses using the correct form of the words in brackets.

1. If you ______ your computer regularly, you ______ able to fill in the forms on this website any more. (not update, not be)
2. If I ______ that pop-up on updating my anti-virus programme seriously, I ______ a virus. (take, not get)
3. If people ______ updates more seriously, there ______ so many data breaches. (take, not be)
4. Our company ______ problems exchanging files if we ______ to newer programme versions. (have, not update)
5. Our software is tested thoroughly. But if errors ______, we ______ security patches immediately. (detect, release)
6. I am sure I ______ out on cool upgrades if I ______ my computer. (miss, not update)
7. People ______ anti-virus software and the latest drivers less if the software ______ free of charge. (download, not be)

3 The IT administrator at your company has made the decision to purchase new computers without consulting you, the manager. Use the phrases from exercise 1 and the notes below to write an email of complaint.

Notes	Your email
Betreff	
Anrede und höflicher Beginn	
Danke für die Informationen bezüglich der gelösten Sicherheitsprobleme	
Verärgerung wegen der Neuanschaffung von Computern, ohne Sie als Geschäftsführer zu konsultieren	
Unakzeptabel, solche wichtigen Entscheidungen ohne den Geschäftsführer zu treffen	
Trotz bester Absichten sind Entscheidungen als Team zu treffen und im besten Interesse der Firma	
Kauf neuer Computer könnte finanzielle Probleme schaffen, u.a. auch durch nötige Software und IT-Spezialisten	
Bessere Lösung muss gefunden werden	
Bitte um Treffen, um dieses Thema zu besprechen	
Höflicher Schluss	

TASK 1 | De-escalating a conflict on the phone → SB p. 214

4 Read the following situations and match them to the phrases below.

1. Somebody is starting to shout and is becoming increasingly aggressive.
2. The problem might be due to a misunderstanding, so you repeat your view on it.
3. At first, your colleague was reluctant to discuss the topic, but now she has opened up.
4. The situation is very distressing, and you prefer to reflect on it before you continue the discussion.
5. You want to express empathy for the other person.
6. It is clear to you that it wasn't the other person's fault, but you wish to resolve the situation now.
7. You are curious about why the situation developed the way it did in the first place.
8. You don't agree with your colleague, but you see his point.
9. It has been entirely your own mistake and you want to apologise for it.
10. You want to share your feelings and express sympathy about this awkward situation.

A I know you didn't mean to do it on purpose. What can we do to tackle this problem?
B This must have been upsetting for you.
C I really appreciate that you are willing to discuss this with me. Thank you for being honest.
D I am terribly sorry. It was all my fault.
E I'd prefer if both of us first calm down before we discuss this any further.
F I wonder how this could have happened.
G As I understand the situtation, this is what caused the problem.
H I need some time to think about it before I can respond to that.
I I understand what you are saying, but I definitely have a different view on this.
J When you told me about it, I felt very upset and sorry for you.

1	2	3	4	5	6	7	8	9	10

FOCUS ON READING → SB pp. 215–217

5 Match the verbs from the word bank with the nouns to form collocations.

complete | prioritise | implement | perform | create | encourage | ensure | diagnose | replace | remedy | increase | minimise

________	any negative impact	________	maintenance tasks
________	optimal functionality	________	operations
________	outdated parts	________	weaknesses
________	reliability	________	problems
________	all assets	________	a collaborative culture
________	clear guidelines	________	smoother workflows

6 Find words and phrases in the text that describe the reasons for and consequences of problems caused by downtime.

Reasons: ____

____

Consequences: ______________________________________

____

____

FOCUS ON MEDIATION → SB pp. 219 – 220

7 Decide if the following situations would more likely be a result of planned downtime or outage times.

Situation	Downtime	Outage
upgrades of machinery		
installation of new machines and devices		
cyberattack		
switching to a new product		
shortages in the supply chain		
construction work in the facility		
operator mistakes		
malfunctioning of the machinery		
power outage		
reconfiguration of the production line		

8 Match the type of cost (A – E) with the business topics. You can use the letters more than once.

A production costs   B labour costs   C maintenance and repair costs

D energy costs   E overhead costs

Cost	Situation
	external repair staff
	rent for the facility
	loss in revenue
	electricity and fuel
	lost productivity
	number of units not produced during downtime
	insurance and taxes
	personnel costs
	spare parts
	overtime for staff resulting from the outage

FOCUS ON LISTENING → SB p. 220

9 Match the levels of the four-sides model of communication with their explanations.

1. factual level | **2.** relationship level | **3.** self-revelation level | **4.** level of appeal

☐ A This refers to the information that is actually given.

☐ B This is how the sender of the information wants the receiver to react.

☐ C It refers to what you want or do not necessarily want to give away about yourself.

☐ D It refers to the connection between the sender and the receiver of the information, which is affected by how they relate to each other.

A26 **10** Listen to the report and fill in the missing words.

1. Michael Jordan said that talent wins games, but teamwork and intelligence win __________.
2. To work together effectively, everyone involved must communicate __________ and __________ with one another.
3. Misunderstandings can be caused by __________.
4. To ensure that a team masters its task with the best success, __________ communication is important.
5. Misunderstandings can easily arise when the sender and receiver interpret a message __________.
6. If you multiply this small misunderstanding many times over, you can see how misunderstandings can __________.
7. If you and your team are sensitive to how messages can be sent and received, you can help to __________ and __________ the situation.
8. Clear communication is important between __________, in customer contact and not least in __________ – it is the __________.

FOCUS ON SPEAKING → SB p. 220

11 Collect words and phrases that express the benefits of an open discussion.

TASK 2 | Discussing a problem face-to-face → SB pp. 221–222

12 Match the best conflict-resolution strategy (A–E) with the situation. You can use the letters more than once.

A competition | B collaboration | C avoidance | D accommodation | E compromise

	although conflicting parties do not agree on their opinions, they come up with an alternative suggestion
	a conflict about deciding the issue would be a waste of time
	although you do not want to be too confrontational, you also want to take a stand
	you were proven wrong and should give in
	you must assert your authority
	the conflicting parties need some time to relax and focus on themselves
	the issue is of little importance
	both sides have good points and nobody is too assertive
	you give up a little ground but also gain a little
	the conflict is buried below the surface as you do not discuss it
	it is an emergency and you as the authority have to implement measures quickly

13 Complete the following replies from Mr Lloyd about the downtime proposed by Cem.

1. I know you did a very good job with introducing new technology. However, ____________________
2. I understand that downtime makes it easier to implement new technology. But ____________________
3. Although I really appreciate that we will have these new machines to replace the obsolete ones, we ____________________
4. You might not know some aspects which are important in the production process. Therefore it is very important to ____________________
5. I know you meant well. In the future, though, ____________________

SCENARIO B

UNDERSTANDING THE SCENARIO → SB pp. 223–224

1 Find the phrases in the email to express the following German statements.

German statement	Phrase
dem Problem auf den Grund gehen	
auf Grund einer Anzahl von Lieferkettenschwierigkeiten	
plötzlicher Anstieg in der Nachfrage	
umfangreiche Nachforschungen anstellen	
den Wareneingangsschein beifügen	
als der Vorfall passierte	
an jdn. mit Informationen herantreten	

2 Complete your colleague Steve's email by putting the verbs in brackets into the correct tense.

Dear Bob,

I ___________ (come) across a serious problem with the delivery of parts for our workshop when ______________ (want) to assemble the bicycles for our Copenhagen consignment this afternoon. We ____________________ (recently, ask) Jenny from the purchasing department to contact *Retro*, the company that ____________ (deliver) chains and gears, to send us the necessary equipment immediately. We _____________ (be) excited to receive the new types of chains, but unfortunately our excitement turned to frustration when we ____________ (open) the package. Actually, when we ____________ (check) the box, we ______________ (discover) that the chains ________________ (miss) entirely.

I ____________________ (now, contact) you as the head of our purchasing department to address this issue asap. We are at a loss as to what to do now. I _____________ (not, have) to tell you how hard we ________________ (work) to prepare this consignment. From our side, we ______________ (not, be) able to meet the deadline of assembling the bicycles by the end of this week. Unfortunately, this is not the first time problems with *Retro* have occurred. We have already had lots of missed deadlines because of them. Last month, we _________________ (not, receive) the required number of saddles, and over Christmas last year the handlebars ________________ (not, send) at all.

We understand that issues like this __________ (arise) from time to time, but it is essential to have a reliable supplier who ____________ (deliver) the required parts on time and in the right condition. Please let me know what we can do to rectify this situation.

Kind regards,

Steve

3 There is one incorrect word in each group. Underline the words and give reasons why they do not fit.

1. revenue reputation assessment collaboration

   Reason: ______________________________

2. recall refund warranty compensation

   Reason: ______________________________

3. liable disappointing inadequate unsatisfactory

   Reason: ______________________________

4. dispute transparency disruptions complication

   Reason: ______________________________

5. satisfaction delay defective unreliable

   Reason: ______________________________

6. mitigate review resolve escalate

   Reason: ______________________________

TASK 1 | Discussing a supplier issue internally → SB p. 225

4 Your colleague has come across the following problems with a supplier. Match the problems (1–6) with the solutions (A–F).

Problems	Solutions
1. The delivery of the WING company is late again. They are really unreliable with their delivery schedules.	A Contact the supplier, explain the experience you had with their customer service and be specific about the issues you encountered.
2. I have read that the supplier is financially unstable and might go out of business.	B Ask if the supplier could deliver at least part of the order now and ask when the other part could be sent.
3. Normally, the ROTOR company delivers on time and in good quality. This time their bolts were of very poor quality.	C We should monitor that and establish a plan to mitigate possible risks. Start to research alternative suppliers.
4. The customer service of this supplier is really poor and they don't provide adequate technical support.	D Review the contract with the supplier. If necessary we should consider terminating the contract and even taking legal action.
5. The supplier has announced that they can't deliver the full quantity of the order by the end of the week.	E Conduct an investigation into the cause of the quality issues. Conduct regular quality checks to ensure that standards will be maintained in the future.
6. The goods have repeatedly arrived late and in incorrect quantities. We now have problems with our own customers who are making us liable.	F Contact them immediately and inquire about the reason for the delay. Ask for a revised delivery schedule and ensure that it aligns with our production needs.

1	2	3	4	5	6

FOCUS ON READING → SB pp. 226 – 228

5 Complete the following word web with information from the reading text.

FOCUS ON LISTENING → SB p. 229

6 Match the definitions with words from the word bank. Then translate the words into German.

stint working | to aspire | to put sb off | tongue-in-cheek | moaner | to be attentive | to grin and bear | not up to scratch | at play | to embarrass

Definition		Translation
1. to accept without wanting to		
2. temporary job		
3. not really good enough		
4. being ironical		
5. to try to accomplish sth		
6. to discourage sb from doing sth		
7. sb who complains a lot unnecessarily		
8. to cause sb to feel uncomfortable		
9. to listen carefully		
10. issues influencing sth		

FOCUS ON SPEAKING → SB p. 229

7 Cross out the words which you consider to be particularly negative when dealing with complaints.

~~judgemental~~ | critical | frustration | praise | genuine interest | problem-solving | gratefulness | politeness | confrontation | to interrupt | to reflect | attitude | aggressive behaviour | disrespect | to acknowledge | assertive | to respect | bias

FOCUS ON MEDIATION → SB pp. 229–231

8 Match the words and phrases from the text to their English equivalents.

1. Versorgungsengpässe
2. Beendigung des Geschäftsverhältnisses
3. der Kosten nicht bewusst sein
4. Beziehungen verschlechtern sich
5. Abweichung hinsichtlich des Materials
6. veränderte Wahrnehmung
7. Unstimmigkeiten
8. Abstimmungsschwierigkeiten
9. Nachhaltigkeitsdiskussionen
10. wertgeschätzter Geschäftspartner

A relationships deteriorate
B valued business partner
C sustainability discussions
D supply shortage
E discrepancies
F not be aware of costs
G changed perception
H deviation on the material side
I coordination difficulties
J termination of business

1	2	3	4	5	6	7	8	9	10

9 Put the joining words from the word bank into the correct category.

at first sight | as a result of | to be honest | perhaps | however | at first glance | in my opinion | possibly | It is too one-sided. | to my mind | consequently | potentially | due to | therefore | unfortunately | It is biased. | unluckily | owing to | despite that | thus | yet

but	so	initially	maybe
______	______	______	______
______	______	______	______
______	______	______	______
because of	**I think**	**sadly**	**It's unfair to say.**
______	______	______	______
______	______	______	______
______	______	______	______

10 Complete the sentences using the phrases from exercise 9.

1. ______________ many modern tools, it is possible to organise a smooth distribution within the supply chain.
2. ____________________, the supplier seemed to be responsible for the errors. ________________, further investigation revealed that mistakes were actually made within our own company.
3. _______________________ to make the lengthy absence of one colleague responsible for the difficulties.
4. __________________, problems can occur when there is some miscommunication between the customer and the supplier.
5. ________________, we should learn from our mistakes to mitigate problems in the future.
6. __________________, we should consider ending our business relationship with this supplier as we have been experiencing recurring issues with our deliveries.

TASK 2 | Writing a formal complaint → SB p. 232

11 Match the sentences 1–7 with A–G to make them more polite.

1. My name is … and I want to complain about the bad quality of your products.	A We value you as an experienced business partner and hope that we can resolve this issue.
2. Your latest product was a big problem for our company.	B Please let me know if there is any additional information that can help to solve this issue.
3. You must look into this matter and give us a solution quickly.	C I regret to inform you that we have had very unsatisfactory experiences with your product.
4. You are a good business partner with whom we want to work on this problem.	D We would like to request an improvement action plan outlining steps that will be taken to …
5. We need an improvement action plan to see what you have done about the problem.	E I kindly request you to take necessary measures to prevent similar problems from happening in the future.
6. I hope you will not make such mistakes again.	F I would appreciate it if you could look into this matter and provide us with a solution as soon as possible.
7. If necessary, we will send you more information on this issue.	G I am writing to you as the … to express my disappointment with products we have received from your company.

1	2	3	4	5	6	7

SCENARIO C

UNDERSTANDING THE SCENARIO → SB pp. 233–234

1 Choose the correct words from the word bank to match the definitions below.

condensation | mould | dampness | mildew | humidity | moisture

1. ____________________ occurs in a building when water or moisture is absorbed by the building material.
2. ____________________ forms when moisture in the air collects on a cooler surface.
3. ____________________ is the black spots on surfaces, corners and poorly ventilated spaces.
4. ____________________ is the presence of water in the air and can cause humidity.
5. ____________________ is a fungus that grows on organic material. It is an early stage of mould.
6. ____________________ is the amount of water vapour in the air.

2 Choose the correct word to complete the sentences.

1. I was satisfied … the quality of the work of the electrician.
   A ☐ about   B ☐ with   C ☐ on   D ☐ by
2. I have attached photos of the damage … this email.
   A ☐ to   B ☐ in   C ☐ with   D ☐ by
3. After a hacker attack, we are warning you … the request for payment from this company.
   A ☐ for   B ☐ about   C ☐ against   D ☐ of
4. Our roofing company specialises … renovating roofs of historic buildings.
   A ☐ on   B ☐ in   C ☐ for   D ☐ by
5. This building engineer is good … managing large construction sites.
   A ☐ at   B ☐ in   C ☐ about   D ☐ on
6. How can we prevent customers … uploading negative reviews on social media sites?
   A ☐ for   B ☐ from   C ☐ about   D ☐ against
7. We are having difficulties getting the building material as timber and cement are … short supply.
   A ☐ about   B ☐ for   C ☐ by   D ☐ in

TASK 1 | Writing a response to a complaint → SB p. 235

3 Do the following adjectives express a positive (😊) or negative (😕) description of people writing and receiving complaints?

relieved	☐	defensive	☐	attentive	☐	thoughtful	☐
distressed	☐	caring	☐	aggressive	☐	patronising	☐
empathetic	☐	patient	☐	dissatisfied	☐	apologetic	☐
disappointed	☐	constructive	☐	calm	☐	respectful	☐

4 Match the following parts of a response to a complaint (1 – 4) with the labels (A – D).

1
Dear Mrs Jackson,

Thank you for your letter regarding the incorrect price we charged for your new windows.

2
We are terribly sorry for the inconvenience and sincerely apologise for the mistake, which seems to have happened because of an error in our sales department.

3
We have taken care of this mistake immediately and of course we will transfer the excess money back to your account as requested. To prevent this from happening again, we have instructed our staff to check orders more carefully.

4
We really apologise for the inconvenience. Please do not hesitate to contact us if there is anything else we can do.

Yours sincerely,
Patricia Smith

A Outline what you are going to do about the problem.		C Apologise sincerely, repeat the problem and offer an explanation.	
B Include a final apology and concluding statement.		D Acknowledge receipt of the complaint.	

FOCUS ON MEDIATION → SB pp. 236 – 237

5 Answer the questions from your new colleague using information from the text. Then act out this dialogue with a partner.

Partner A: Why do we have to respond to complaints within 24 hours?

Partner B: It is a good quality feature to ____

____.

Partner A: What should I do about a loud and aggressive customer?

Partner B: Approach the customer with ____

____.

Partner A: What should I ask or tell the upset customer?

Partner B: ____.

Partner A: Should I tell the customer about the problem?

Partner B: Yes, of course. Customers often ____

____.

Partner A: How can I finish the complaint-handling process with the customer?

Partner B: Summarise ____

____.

FOCUS ON READING → SB pp. 238 – 240

6 Choose the correct answer.

1. Surface condensation is caused by moisture-laden air coming into contact with a …
   - A ☐ hot surface.
   - B ☐ dry surface.
   - C ☐ cold surface.
   - D ☐ wet surface.
2. Relative humidity is the amount of moisture in the air compared to …
   - A ☐ the temperature.
   - B ☐ what the air can hold at that temperature.
   - C ☐ the pressure.
   - D ☐ the altitude.
3. Dew is the moisture that has …
   - A ☐ evaporated into the air.
   - B ☐ condensed on surfaces due to saturation of the air.
   - C ☐ frozen into tiny crystals on surfaces.
   - D ☐ been absorbed by plants.
4. Modern properties have more problems with condensation because they …
   - A ☐ have more leaks and draughts.
   - B ☐ are built with less sturdy materials.
   - C ☐ have less natural ventilation.
   - D ☐ are affected by climate change.
5. Diffusion is the process of moisture …
   - A ☐ condensing on surfaces.
   - B ☐ moving around the home.
   - C ☐ evaporating from surfaces.
   - D ☐ being absorbed by surfaces.
6. Which factor does not contribute to the condensation of water building up on surfaces?
   - A ☐ high humidity of indoor air
   - B ☐ poor ventilation
   - C ☐ low temperature of the walls / surfaces
   - D ☐ heating
7. What should you do if you already have mould growth in your home?
   - A ☐ Leave it alone.
   - B ☐ Increase humidity levels.
   - C ☐ Take steps to have it removed.
   - D ☐ Paint over it.

FOCUS ON LISTENING → SB p. 240

A27 **7** Listen to the audio and complete the table.

Why to DIY: Dealing with mould and condensation	
Health	Danger to those with: ____________ Symptoms: ____________
Protective clothing	rubber gloves, dust mask, ____________
Liquids	• special mould and mildew ____________ • mixture of normal household bleach and water: ________ part bleach to ________ parts water • mild ____________ with a combination of water and ____________
Steps to remove mould / mildew	1. remove and dispose of any mouldy items or materials ____________ 2. spray the area with some ____________ 3. scrub the affected area with your ____________ 4. regularly clean the ____________ and use ____________ 5. let the area ____________ thoroughly for a day or two
Prevention	• keep things clean • make sure all areas where moisture can potentially gather are well ____________ • keep ____________ open during the day • avoid placing large items of furniture against ____________ • invest in a ____________ • install a humidity-sensing ____________ • consider using ____________
Benefits of clay plaster	• looks ____________ • buffers ____________ in room humidity • creates ____________ • helps minimise the ____________

FOCUS ON WRITING → SB p. 241

8 Write a short description for how you would carry out the task of wallpapering a wall. The words from the word bank below will help you.

wallpaper | paste / adhesive | layer | ladder | rubber roller / brush

____

____

____

____

____

TASK 2 | Discussing a problem on site → SB pp. 242–243

9 Your company has guidelines for meeting clients on the building site. Complete the guidelines using the words from the word bank.

focus | have | keep | show | find | avoid | explain | use | provide | establish

Tips for meeting clients

- ______________ that you have expertise in the field of building and renovating.
- ______________ industry jargon, i.e. excessive technical terms.
- ______________ on the client and listen to their wishes to prevent possible problems.
- ______________ out how you will communicate with the client – via email, phone or on site.
- ______________ how often you will meet the client to show work progress.
- ______________ what items are included in the invoice.
- ______________ a clear and concise contract and explain it to the customer.
- ______________ technology to illustrate the ideas to your client, e.g. 3D designs.
- ______________ your client engaged in the construction process in case there are changes.
- ______________ information in case there are delays in the building process.

10 Look at the list of dos and don'ts when dealing with complaints on a building site and mark the correct columns.

Do	Don't	
		… be afraid of customer complaints.
		… ask questions to determine the core issue of the complaint.
		… make unrealistic promises to clients.
		… decide what to do about the customer complaint.
		… be frustrated about the complaint.
		… talk your client down with industry-specific words.
		… appreciate the feedback, even though it is a complaint.
		… show off and tell the client how experienced and impeccable you are.
		… reach out to your client to find out if the problem is fully resolved.
		… jump to conclusions about why the problem has happened.

EXAM PRACTICE

Teil 1 Hörverstehen → SB p. 246

A28 1 Listen to the podcast and select the correct answers for the questions below. There can be more than one correct option.

1. What mistakes do people often make in conflictual situations?

A ☐ being aggressive
B ☐ expecting too much
C ☐ not listening properly
D ☐ not seeing the other person's perspective
E ☐ only looking at the situation through their own framework of understanding

2. Why might a person say something provocative in a situation of conflict?

A ☐ they want to start a conflict
B ☐ they are not very self-confident
C ☐ they are extremely aggressive by nature
D ☐ they have been advised to insist on their own standpoint
E ☐ they think they have heard something provocative aimed at them

3. What is the effect of starting a conversation by being very certain of your own point of view?

A ☐ creating a conflict
B ☐ not gaining any more clarity
C ☐ tending not to ask questions
D ☐ preventing a situation of conflict
E ☐ convincing others of your opinion

4. How may we "untangle the threads" in a conflictual conversation?

A ☐ call in a mediator
B ☐ fight back when we feel attacked
C ☐ ascertain our position and articulate it clearly
D ☐ write down all of the points raised and discuss them one by one
E ☐ engage with the other person and find out what they are thinking and feeling

Teil 2 Schriftliche Rezeption → SB pp. 246–247

2 Match the words and phrases from the text with their German equivalents.

1. occurrence (l. 2)	A Streitigkeit, Auseinandersetzung
2. clash (l. 3)	B unvoreingenommen
3. dispute (l. 11)	C Vorfall, Ereignis
4. to assess (l. 24)	D letztes Mittel
5. unbiased (l. 27)	E bewerten
6. to aggravate (l. 30)	F Konflikt, Aufeinanderprallen
7. to boost (l. 41)	G verstärken, steigern
8. last resort (l. 46)	H verschlechtern, verschlimmern

Teil 3 Schriftliche Kommunikation → SB p. 248

3 Use the following words and phrases to respond to the manager's concerns by acknowledging the changes, stating possible consequences and offering solutions.

1. to change workplaces of managers and executives / to create discomfort → to retain executives

____

____

____

____

2. heavy workload / to feel stressed / new routines and tasks → to provide training / supervision

____

____

____

____

3. to coordinate different teams / conflicts → new strategy / to mediate conflicts

____

____

____

____

4. to reduce workforce / resistance of trade unions → to understand changes / to avoid layoffs

____

____

____

____

5. to reorganise processes / to neglect one branch → corporate policy / transparency / communication

____

____

____

____

Teil 4 Mediation → SB pp. 248–249

4 Complete the email to the team manager with information from the text about why mediation might offer a solution to the problem between the staff.

Dear Mr Fairchild,

I have found some information on why mediation could be a solution to the tense situation among our staff members that you mentioned to me yesterday.

With mediation, we would have a ________________ situation. When the disputing parties start a ____________________________, the needs and concerns of both parties _______________________ and nobody __________________.

Instead of having latent conflicts and long-lasting ___________________________, a mediator who has been called in on time can ________________ an escalation of conflicts and _________________________ instead. In this way, a mediator helps to find solutions ______________ and _______________. __________________ are released and ______________________________ relaxes. This has the advantage that the ______________, _______________ and ______________ of the parties involved can concentrate on __________________________________. Moreover, relationships are maintained because mediation prevents their ___________________________.

Solving problems together opens up an understanding of other people's ____________________ and can ________________ communication in the long run. Finally, costs are kept low because hiring a mediator is _________________________ and _____________________ than taking the matter ________________. I hope this information convinces you to solve the conflict among our staff with the help of a mediator.

Yours sincerely,

Teil 5 Rollenbasierte Stellungnahme → SB p. 249

5 Complete the statements on introducing a training course in mediation using your own ideas.

1. I don't see why ____
   ____.
2. Personally speaking, ____
   ____.
3. As far as I am concerned, ____
   ____.
4. There is no doubt that ____
   ____.
5. Wouldn't you say that ____
   ____?